T

July 21, 1985

To Oscar —

— Welcome aboard!

Pete Rogers cns

TRAGEDY
Working for God in

Revised and Expanded Edition

The Habersham Corporation

NEW ORLEANS

IS MY PARISH

the Streets of New Orleans

Peter V. Rogers, O. M. I.

The Habersham Corporation
333 St. Charles Avenue
New Orleans, LA 70130

Library of Congress Cataloging in Publication Data

Rogers, Peter V
    Tragedy is my parish.

    Autobiography.
    1. Rogers, Peter V. 2. Catholic Church—
Clergy—Biography. 3. Clergy—Louisiana—New
Orleans—Biography. 4. New Orleans—Biography.
5. Chaplains, Police—Louisiana—New Orleans—
Biography. I. Title.
BX4705.R648A34   282′.092′4 [B]   78-25896
ISBN 0-02-604390-4

First Habersham Printing 1983

Printed in the United States of America

*This book is dedicated with respect
and with affection to my father,
Peter V. Rogers, Sr.
His entire life has been one of
courage, of faith, and of deep love
for his God, his country,
and his family.*

Contents

Acknowledgments

THE AUTHOR WISHES TO THANK everyone who, in one way or another, gave the inspiration and the "go" for this book: the men and women of the New Orleans police and fire departments. Special thanks to all who helped bring it to completion, especially my patient and talented secretary, Frances Roberson; and so many others, including researchers Maria-Kay and Irene Chetta (a policewoman for twenty years). Also, Rev. J. Nicholas, O.M.I., Supt. Bill McCrossen of the Fire Department, Supt. Clarence Giarrusso of the Police Department, and Andrea Camps, Ph.D. Many thanks also to Deputy Chief Fred Reiser, Jules Killelea, Maj. Lloyd Poisenot, Sgt. Bob Childress, and many others, living and dead, all of whom gave inspiring help. For the use of photographs, I want to thank G. E. Arnold, George Haber, Richard Blackmon, Frank Methe, the *Times-Picayune* and the *States-Item* newspapers.

By Way of Introduction

I AM A CATHOLIC PRIEST.

In addition, I wear the badge of Chaplain, New Orleans Police and Fire Departments.

And, believe me, I wear it proudly.

Because I *am* proud of my men and women: 1,400 police officers and 1,000 firefighters of the city of New Orleans. And, in reality, this is *their* story. And I am proud to be some part of it. Sure, as with every police or fire department in the nation, we have some bad people. These few are neither condoned nor coddled—and when discovered, must be rooted out.

Sure, there are some who are found in church only when they are pallbearers for a fallen buddy or when they themselves are carried in with the American flag draped over them.

And that makes my job even more challenging.

I am more than distressed, however, with the sweeping, general accusations leveled against the "brutal bad-guy cop"—the favorite subject in rhetoric, prose, and TV over the recent years. The vast majority of good officers and firemen and their families must silently suffer.

And so, I write this book for two reasons. The first is to state publicly how proud I am of the majority of our men, women, and their children. Within these pages are some of the events that have happened to me—and to them— over the past twelve years. I've changed only some names and places now and then to avoid embarrassment to some and to protect all concerned.

My second reason for writing this book is the hope that some young—or maybe not-so-young—man, teetering on the brink of the Great Decision—what to do with his life— might find an added reason to saddle up and ride with my congregation, the Oblates of Mary Immaculate.

And then on one happy tomorrow I might silently and proudly watch as the gold badge, "Chaplain, New Orleans Police and Fire Departments," is pinned on *him*.

Nightly, my prayer is that the good Lord will protect my very special "parishioners" from every harm—physical and moral.

TRAGEDY IS MY PARISH

CHAPTER 1

Shoot-Out at the Dream Girl

3:52 A.M.

THE WINDSHIELD WIPERS on the Ford Cobra slammed from side to side with a staccato "whack—whack—whack" rhythm as I turned left on Canal Street and headed toward the river. It was not raining, but the humidity and a light fog made the noisy wipers a must. I glanced at my watch; 3:52 A.M.—just twenty minutes since Headquarters had called. Canal Street was just about deserted, as if bracing itself for another hectic day. Car 30 and the police chaplain were rolling again.

New Orleans, Louisiana: city of charm, lore, history— and often, violence. The Crescent City, sitting four feet below sea level, is often depressingly humid, but on that early morning of March 22, it was especially bad. The morning sky was clouded with a light mist from the Mississippi. Exhaust fumes from a fleet of tourist buses combined with the sight and smell of gunsmoke which was hanging heavy in the air. On the streets of New Orleans, this is a formula both ominous and sinister.

The 500 block of Canal Street—just a few blocks from the Mississippi River—was the scene. Sgt. Joe Delery of the New Orleans Police Department's First District mopped his brow.

"Jeez—this reminds me of 'Nam! That guy must be something else!"

The screaming "wa-wa's" of sirens could be heard as more squad cars screeched to a halt near the Dream Girl

Bar & Lounge. Some of the police were crouched in front with guns drawn and, on command, moved around to the rear. Others were being briefed by their rank.

"He's sitting at the last table on the left. He's been hit. Looks like he's bleeding pretty good—but he's loaded for bear."

"What's he usin', Sergeant?"

"Well, he's got a double shotgun, plus a handpiece, and God knows how much ammo. Some Swede—a sailor that was sitting at a front table—has been hit, but not bad."

It was now 3:30 in the morning, but no one really keeps time in New Orleans. Even at that hour, a sizable crowd began to gather on Canal Street as shots zinged in and out of the bar. Curious nightclubbers, eyes shining with anticipation, were watching from behind lamp posts and cars: another New Orleans show—and no cover charge for this one! Drifters and winos, eyes bleary and heavy with booze, were hiding behind trash cans, squinting through the smoke and fog, enjoying a brief diversion from their routine of boredom. A few tourists, eyes wide with fear, were huddled together for protection and watched from a distance as more armed police in battle helmets took their positions around the sleazy bar.

Capt. Dan Pearson, Commander of the First, pulled up and called his sergeant over. "What's it all about, Joe?"

"Jeez, Cap—it's a screwed-up deal. From what I can put together, a guy named Nick Stoppio is the owner of this dump. They say he was trying to make one of the barmaids, a gal named Linda. Her husband found out about it, had a few drinks, armed himself, and went hunting— for Stoppio. Lucky for him Stoppio isn't here; so now he's shooting at us and anyone who comes near him."

The captain looked thoughtful. "Yeah, I remember Stoppio. He's that no-goodnik who used to hustle young broads off the farms in Mississippi and Alabama. He'd promise

2

them a big job, bring them here, and then get them to
turn tricks."

"Yeah," said the sergeant. "That's him. He owns a couple of joints like this around the French Quarter. Nobody,
but *nobody,* would miss him if someone did shoot him—I
guarantee."

The sergeant, who weighed in at about 250 pounds, was
perspiring. He mopped his brow and the band inside his
blue-and-white battle helmet emblazoned with the gold
crest of the New Orleans Police Department. "We've got
the place surrounded, Cap. It's just a matter of time."
Looking thoughtful for a moment, he said quietly,
"Y'know, that kid in there looks about eighteen years old—
same age as one of mine. I know if Stoppio was messing
around with *my* old lady—"

Captain Pearson looked over to the bar. "Has anyone
tried to talk to him?"

"Can't get near him. He's sitting way in the back, at the
last table, and is shooting at anything that moves. Probably
jittery as hell."

The captain, a veteran of sixteen years with the department, moved to his car and picked up his radio mike. No
harm in trying, he thought, before someone is killed.

"Car 120 to Headquarters."

"Headquarters, 120—get Father Rogers on the phone
and tell him we need him in the 500 block of Canal. I'll
meet him there."

The radio crackled back, "That's 10-04, sir."

Driving down Canal I soon saw the blue police lights
flashing in the 500 block, and I pulled the Ford up on the
neutral ground and stopped beside Car 120. I tucked the
small black kit which contains the holy oils and the ritual
of the Church under my arm. The kit also carries a stole,
cotton, and holy water—plus such nonliturgical items as a

3

package of cigarettes, a bottle of Murine (to soothe a fire-man's smoke-blinded eyes), a couple of packs of gum, plus a few nickels for emergency phone calls. Walking over, I nodded to the captain.

"Hi, Dan. What have we?"

"Padre, there's a suspect in there whose wife has been—allegedly—mistreated by the owner of the place. He came looking for the owner, a man named Stoppio who wasn't around; and now he's taking on the whole police depart-ment. There are five of our people on this side of the bar trying to talk to him, but he just keeps pumping away. I was wondering if—"

"Anyone know his name?"

"One of the men inside said it was Mike Mellon or Nelson—but we're not sure."

The sergeant went to his car and returned with a bullet-proof vest. "Better slip this on, Chaplain. It's chilly out to-night."

"That doesn't protect the brains, Joe," I said, chuckling. "And I think that's where I most need the help!" With the black kit under my arm, I began to walk slowly toward the door of the Dream Girl Bar & Lounge.

"Damn fool," muttered the sergeant; but as his eyes met mine, there was a strange look in the old cop's eyes. I crossed the sidewalk and entered the bar. This place will never bag the 'Holiday Award,' I thought, as I entered the dirty saloon.

The front part of the bar was so filled with gunsmoke that at first it was almost impossible to see, and my eyes stung. Crouching down, I made my way over to two police-men who were hunched behind the corner of the bar with drawn .38s. They gave the same version of what was going on as the captain had.

"O.K. Do me a favor and hold your fire. I want to see if he'll listen to me; maybe even talk to me. Cover me if you want, but shoot only if you have to. Will you do that for me?"

The younger of the two looked at me. "You kidding? This guy's nuts, Father. He's already hit a sailor. And *you* better get down."

"Let's give it a try. Is his name Mellon?"

"Someone said Mike Mellon; husband of a gal named Linda who works here."

All two hundred pounds of me stood up as tall as I could, and I slowly began to walk toward the rear of the bar. A large picture of a nude woman on a wall calendar smiled down at me. A thought flew through my head: I'll bet that's the "dream girl" they named this dump after. She pointed her big twin breasts right at me—and ten yards away Mike Mellon pointed his big, twin-barreled shotgun right at my stomach.

"Mike? Can you hear me? My name is Father Rogers— Father Rogers—. I'm a Catholic priest and just want to talk to you. Can I sit down and talk with you?—I want to help you, Mike. I don't want to see you hurt—O.K.?"

Silence.

God, why was everything so silent all of a sudden. I could visualize the young cop back at the bar holding his breath—and waiting.

"Mike Mellon—it's Father Rogers, a *priest*. I want to talk to you for a minute."

More god-awful silence.

I continued the slow walk toward the back table, and then I saw him clearly. He was young—young and scared. His face was very pale, and through the haze and the smoke he was peering at me down the barrel of that deadly 12-gauge shotgun.

Another thought flashed through my mind: This is the script of an old John Wayne movie—two men walking slowly toward each other. A sudden movement. One drops.

My lips formed the words and my heart joined them in the best Act of Contrition I ever made: "O my God, I am heartily sorry for my sins—"

The silence was ominous. Scary.

The officers in the front of the bar aimed their revolvers at an imaginary postage stamp between the gunman's eyes, their fingers resting lightly on the triggers.

As I got closer to Mellon, I continued to talk soothingly to him. I was about five feet away when his eyes opened wide, as if he were just seeing me. He stared at me for about ten seconds, then suddenly jumped up and, holding the gun upright like a processional candle, screamed in a delirious chant, *"Introibo ad altare Dei!"*

An electric shock went through me. And then I smiled. I knew we had him.

In a quiet, firm voice, I responded, *"Ad Deum, qui laetificat juventutem meam."* I slowly approached him, keeping my eyes on his. From a wound on his left cheek, blood spurted down his face and onto his shirt, making it gory. There were six or seven empty beer cans on the table. I slowly extended my hand.

"Hi, Mike. I'm Father Pete. Can I sit down?"

The frightened youth's eyes darted to the front of the bar, to the dozen armed officers there warily looking at him with cold, cold eyes.

"Nobody's going to hurt you, Mike. I promise you that. I want you to come with me to the rectory where I live. It's just a few blocks from here. I want to have a cup of coffee with you and get you cleaned up a little bit. And I want to have your wife Linda meet us there."

The glazed and fear-filled eyes of the young man with blood gushing down his cheek lit up when he heard the name Linda. In a voice just above a whisper he said, "They're gonna bust me, though. They're gonna bury me forever. I think I killed a cop."

I tried to keep my voice as calm and soothing as I could. "No, Mike, you didn't kill anyone. You slightly wounded a civilian—let me help you now. As a matter of fact, I'm the only one who *can* help you."

Sitting down beside him at the table, I continued to speak softly, earnestly, giving the reasons why resistance would mean death. Mike was listening, but his eyes and his gun watched for any movement in the front.

Ten minutes later the gunman said, "O.K., we'll go to your place. I'll talk to you—only you, get that? But if they try anything, you'll get it first—and then I'll blast my own goddamn head off." He placed the end of the shotgun to his throat, about an inch above his Adam's apple. "Tell them that!"

"Mike, I promise they won't touch you. Let's get out of here and go where it's quiet, and we'll talk. Then we'll decide what to do and how I can best help you—and Linda."

After a few more minutes of deliberation, Mike slowly rose from the table. He put the revolver in his belt, stuffed the shells into the jacket pocket, and holding the shotgun to his throat, said, "Let's go."

We began a slow walk back through the littered barroom—a man in a white collar walking close beside a skinny, frightened kid who firmly held a fully loaded, deadly shotgun to his throat, his eyes darting from policeman to policeman.

I'd better not put him in my car, I thought. He just might slip or stumble getting in with that shotgun, and one of us might get hurt. We'd better walk it.

Outside the bar I saw Captain Pearson coming toward us, and I quickly called out to him, "Mike and I are going to take a little walk over to the rectory, Captain. Would you get hold of Linda, his wife, and bring her there? She lives at 2181½ Magazine. Have the men let us through. When things calm down a bit, I'll call you. Right?" And I gave the veteran policeman a large wink.

And so, at 4:45 on that very humid morning in New Orleans, a young man and a priest, followed slowly by a score of policemen and detectives with guns in their hands, began the nine-block walk to Our Lady of Guadalupe rectory. Even for New Orleans, it was a strange parade. I didn't know it then, but a supermarksman had been called to the scene and was positioned behind a car directly across the street from the church house.

Ten minutes later our strange procession arrived at the rectory on Rampart Street, and then Mike Mellon and I began to talk.

One hour and fifteen minutes later the officers outside saw the front door of the rectory open. Holding the shotgun and a .25 revolver, I called to them. Mike Mellon and his sobbing Linda were at my side. His wound had been washed and cleaned, and I had given him a fresh shirt, which was about five sizes too big for him.

"Captain, Mike has decided to turn himself in. I'll drive him down to Central Lockup if it's O.K. with you."

Sergeant Delery stepped forward. Mike put his hands out in front of him, and the cuffs snapped in place. Another officer patted him down, finding nothing but $1.17, a comb—and a photo of Linda.

Dan Pearson said, "O.K., Father, you can ride him over to CLU. We'll be right behind."

Mike's eyes were shining as he got into my car. "Thanks, Padre. Stick with me, and, like you said, we'll make it together."

As he took Mike's weapons and shells from me, Sergeant Delery whispered, "Hey, Chaplain. What was that he shouted at you when he first saw you in the bar?"

"That, Joe, was Latin. As a young kid, Mike was kicked around various orphanages all over the country, wherever his mother felt like getting off the bus. One of those was a Catholic place called St. Brendan's, in Missouri. He liked the priest there—the only real friend, apparently, that he ever had up to that time. He became an altar boy at the orphanage, and he never forgot the first line of the old Latin mass. When he saw me tonight in the bar, I guess I reminded him of that priest, the priest who was his only friend—the only one who ever helped him. God works in funny ways, Joe."

"What do the words mean?"

"They're in the Bible, and they mean, 'I will go to the altar of God.' And I have a feeling that very soon Mike will do just that! In fact, he started tonight!"

CHAPTER 2

The Streets Cry Out

10:15 A.M.

I'LL ALWAYS REMEMBER THAT DAY when I was sworn in as Chaplain of the New Orleans Police and Fire Departments. There were a lot of people assembled at 10:15 on the morning of May 17, 1965 in the offices of Victor Schiro, Mayor of New Orleans. And I was nervous. In fact, scared.

Almost like Ordination day, I mused.

Joseph I. Giarrusso and Arthur Hyde, the chiefs of the police and the fire departments, respectively, were there, along with Councilman Joe DiRosa; Rev. Bob Shirley, the Protestant chaplain; and a whole flock of top politicos.

I raised my right hand and softly repeated after the mayor: "I, Father Peter Rogers, do solemnly swear—"

The main reason for my nervousness, I suppose, was that I really didn't know *what* I was getting into.

The history of the Catholic chaplains in New Orleans has been a long and distinguished one. I knew that it all began back in 1918 when the Oblates of Mary Immaculate were invited here by Archbishop Dennis Shaw, who had previously known the Oblates and their work when he was bishop in San Antonio, Texas. After being named archbishop of New Orleans, he offered the Oblate Fathers direction of the historical St. Louis Cathedral, which was in deplorable condition and desperately in need of repair, plus the two "filial" chapels, St. Mary's Italian church on Chartres Street, with the famous Ursuline Convent as the rectory, and the unnamed little church on the corner of North Rampart and Conti streets.

I had done a little digging and found out the reason why it was unnamed. The Dominican Fathers had had charge of the ancient little church, first known only as the "burial chapel," and later called St. Anthony of Padua. In 1917 the Dominicans were given a new and larger parish on Canal Street in New Orleans. They were also given permission to take with them the name of their former parish, St. Anthony, thus leaving the old church without a name—and without priests to staff it.

In 1904 there also existed a famous (or infamous) plot of real estate in New Orleans known as Storyville. It was located behind the church on Basin Street. To protect the lives and property of the fair damsels, madams, and pimps in Storyville (for Storyville was the prostitution district of the bawdy city) the fire department had built Engine House 13.

Fr. Jules Bornes was the first Oblate pastor of the church, and on quiet summer evenings he would walk over and chat with the firefighters in their engine house. They enjoyed this kind and good-humored man, and it was natural, when a fireman was injured or killed while on a call, that they would summon their friend Father Bornes, and he always responded. In 1919 he was officially named the chaplain of the New Orleans Fire Department.

The New Orleans Police Department, with eighty percent of its men at that time of the Catholic faith, followed suit a few years later, and so the tradition began that whoever was pastor of Our Lady of Guadalupe Church, the new name given by Father Bornes to the old St. Anthony's, was also chaplain of both departments.

Following Father Bornes's retirement in 1941, Fr. Joseph Laux was named the second Oblate pastor and chaplain. In his nineteen years as chaplain, Father Laux, a native of San Antonio, Texas, piled up a tremendous record with the men of both departments.

"He was completely dedicated," recalls Deputy Fire

Chief Edward O'Brien, Sr. Father Laux will never be forgotten by the veterans of both departments.

Fr. Joe Laux was transferred in 1961 to Del Rio, Texas, as pastor of Sacred Heart Church, and was succeeded at Guadalupe by Fr. John Sauvaugeau, O.M.I., a French-Canadian from Montreal, who joined the Southern Oblate Province in 1938. He worked with the Spanish-speaking in various parishes in Texas and came to New Orleans in 1961. While here, he obtained his doctorate in languages from Tulane University and in 1965 was transferred to teach at Our Lady of the Lake College in San Antonio.

And then I came along.

As I stood there in the mayor's office that day, I wondered what I was getting into. I knew that most large metropolitan cities like New York, Chicago, Boston, and San Francisco had a police and fire chaplain—but what did one do?

Listening to the brief speeches of welcome made by Mayor Schiro and the other dignitaries, I looked down at the gold chaplain's shield on my black lapel. Was it just a pretty toy? Was it an empty title, signifying only that I was now the city's official invocation-giver at police graduations?

Not knowing what really was ahead, I took a second oath that morning. One that only my God heard.

I promised to try to be of service to the men and women of these two departments. Day or night, rain or shine, wherever and whenever and in whatever way I was needed—I would try to be there.

Just prior to the ceremony, I was chatting with Jules Ursin, an old and respected cop. He looked me in the eye and said, "Father, welcome to the department. We need you, and you'll need us. You won't find us all in nice polished pews singing hymns in church, but you will be with us in the streets, where often there is blood and vomit and screams and suffering. You won't hear any 'Thou's' and 'Thy's' in the streets, but in their own language, the streets are crying out. They need a man of God—welcome."

And my silent promise that morning was to try always to be God's street priest.

CHAPTER 3

Accent: New Orleans

11:45 P.M.

DID YOU EVER STOP TO THINK what fascinating things *radios* are?

From the insides of even a tiny radio set one can listen to a broadcast from the most remote corner of the world; hear the most beautiful concert music; tune in the Neronian voice of a new, crazed dictator declaring war; pick up the throbbing sobs of a soap opera; or catch the voice of a man walking on the moon. A radio can bring messages of love or hate or war or peace. And in the case of the police radio, messages of danger and excitement and drama and death. I've even seen the police radio used as a weapon— to ram a suspect's teeth down his throat after the thug pulled a knife on a cop who had stopped him for a traffic violation.

The police chaplain's rectory, Our Lady of Guadalupe in New Orleans, has two police radios and one fire radio. In my car, Car 30, there is another two-way VHF police radio. They are *never* off.

The New Orleans Police Department receives an average of 1,300 calls every day; about 40,000 calls per month! The fire department, about 300 calls daily. The complaints range from "There's a snake under my house!" to a long beep followed by "Any car in the area—it's a signal 30. A triple homicide at 2978½ Burgundy—on a Code 3."

In my office, whether I'm banging away at the typewriter or trying to help a couple whose marriage is in trouble, or working at any of the thousands of daily details that are part of any parish priest's life, or opening the mountain of daily mail that comes to the Shrine of St. Jude, or chatting on the telephone, I keep one ear on the steady, no-nonsense voice of the police dispatcher.

From my first moment as chaplain, I have never ceased to be amazed at the "cool" displayed by this team of five men and women dispatchers who sit around a large, round table on the second floor at Headquarters and direct an entire army.

They calmly send a huge fleet of patrol cars, motorcycles, emergency units, tow trucks, and unmarked cars on the most dangerous missions. Dispatchers have a myriad of details to watch over. The entire city is divided up into eight police districts, and there are separate radio channels handling those districts, with one dispatcher handling two or three districts. In addition, the AI (Accident Investigation), the FAS (Felony Action Squad), the Urban Squad (patrolling the ten housing projects), the Detective Bureau, the Homicide Bureau, the Vice Squad, and eleven other special departments are in on various channels.

Within each district, there are various zones to which a special police unit is assigned. The dispatcher must know not to send Car 808 to 1920 South Clairborne Street, because that is 807's zone.

Dispatchers also operate the national and local computers which sit like TV sets in front of each person's station in the dispatcher's room. In a matter of seconds, the dispatcher can relay requested information to an officer in the street who has stopped a suspicious car. In an amazingly short time, the officer knows whether or not the car is stolen, to whom and at what address it is registered, and its serial number.

These cool officers also keep a vigilant eye on each patrol car's "10-40" (coffee or lunch break); give permission for them to take a break; and note how long the car has been on the break. It is the dispatcher's role to keep the air clear during a high-speed chase and to direct other units where and how to head off the fleeing vehicle. The dispatcher must know the one-man patrol cars and the cars with two men riding—and sometimes this changes daily. In time of special danger, it is the dispatcher's job to find back-up units to race to the aid of an "officer in trouble"— the dreaded 108 call. It is the dispatcher who usually gets the chaplain when there is a "signal red"—a crisis situation.

One of the amazing things to me is that the vocal expression of these men and women never changes. No panic, no screaming, no shouting—even in the most critical and dangerous moments. They are cool, professional, and crisp, whether sending a car to a scene where a woman is being attacked in a dark alley or telling one of the three-wheelers to pick up some "po-boy" sandwiches for Headquarters.

It is also the dispatcher's duty to mark up "dispositions"—the manner and result of an officer's handling of a case to which he was assigned. The dispatcher must prod forgetful officers into getting that information in before they go off duty. All their conversations are taped, to protect both the citizens and the police department, should future lawsuits arise. All in all, the dispatchers are the brainwaves of a vast city-wide corps of the crack troops that are ready and waiting to move against the criminal and his crime.

But there is the lighter side. One night, not too long ago, a car in the Sixth District answered an alleged rape call (Signal 27-42). After investigation, the dispatcher asked the first car on the scene if he needed the crash truck (the emergency unit). Without a trace of sarcasm, Car 603 replied, "That's 10-04, sir. The lady claims she's been raped forty-two times."

There was dead silence for a long minute, and then someone, somewhere, opened his mike and let out a long, low wolf whistle. Loud laughter and chuckles could be heard from many different radios until the dispatcher, cool and all business, snapped to the whistler, "You're 10-03, sir!" (You're out of order!) And after a few seconds, he added, "And so was *she!*"

One of the oldest police radio stories is handed down from the early days of radio. A policeman was told by his dispatcher that there was a report that a dead horse was in front of 523 Tchoupitoulas Street. That particular officer was not a Rhodes scholar and had trouble with spelling; so when he arrived at the scene, he dragged the horse around the corner and then radioed his dispatcher.

"Yes, sir, there's a dead horse here, but he's not on that street you gave me."

"Where is he?" the dispatcher asked.

"He's in front of 510 Camp Street—C–A–M–P!"

I'll never forget the first—the very first—emergency call that I received on my police radio. I had been sworn in as chaplain only two days earlier. It was late at night, about 11:45, and I was about to switch off the light in the office and head upstairs when the radio barked: "Headquarters to Car 30—Car 30—"

"Hey, he's calling me!" I thought.

"Headquarters to Car 30."

After a moment or two of shock I grabbed the microphone that rested on the side of the police radio and loudly shouted, "This is Car 30."

But I was talking "over" someone else, and as a result, neither of us could be heard. The cool voice of the dispatcher continued, "Go ahead, Car 703. Someone cut you off."

It seemed like an eternity before 703 passed along some information about an ADT (burglar alarm) going off at

Sears on Gentilly. Then someone else came in, asking for a 10-40 at the Burger King. When they finally finished, I tried to keep my voice steady as I wheezed, "Car 30 to Headquarters."

After what seemed a very long time, the dispatcher responded, "Car 30—you got Channel C, Charlie?"

I looked at the radio in my office. "No, just A and B—but I've got Channel C in my car. Can you wait?"

"I'll be here till seven in the morning."

Can you wait? What a dumb thing to say, I thought as I raced upstairs to get the car keys from my suit coat pocket. They weren't there. Where did I leave them?

Sweating, I ran back down to the office, after checking the kitchen and the dining room, feeling that the whole world would explode if I didn't get that call—*fast!* Books and papers flew off the office desk, and I finally found the car keys under the latest copy of the diocesan paper, *The Clarion Herald*.

I dashed out to my car, which was parked in front of the rectory, turned on the ignition, and immediately picked up the mike. Breathlessly but triumphantly I called, "Car 30 to Channel C." But again I was talking over someone already on the air and ruined still another conversation. After things were settled, in a quiet little voice, I repeated the call.

"Father," the dispatcher said, "we've got an urgent message for the wife of a 26—er—the wife of a policeman. Command Desk wants you to deliver the message—in person. Seems the lady's mother passed away at her home in Alabama this evening, and we just got the word. Her husband, the 26, is out of town for three days on a police assignment. Would you be able to break the news to the lady that her mother has died?"

"10-04. Sure will. Where does she live?"

"At 1181 Levee Street, which is right off Downman Road—are you 10-04 on that?"

My hand gripped the mike—hard. So hard that had it been made of putty it would have had the shape of a long strand of spaghetti.

"Wait till I write that down." I fished out some paper and a pen. The pen didn't write. I found a pencil in the glove compartment.

"Sorry. Pen's out of ink!"

"That's 10-04, sir."

"1181 Levee—which is off Diamond Road, right?"

"10-04. Know where Downman Road is?"

"Negative. I'm new at this."

A slight chuckle came from the veteran dispatcher. "Yeah, I know, Father. Well, do you know where Gentilly Road is?—No, wait, I'll tell you—"

I broke in. "Can I get my coat and collar? Inside?" I felt like a little boy asking permission from the teacher to go to the toilet.

But the dispatcher was most understanding. "Yeah, sure. Don't break your neck. We'll continue to work this on Channel C—that's the conversation channel."

"10-04. Thank you." I got out of the car and raced back to the front door of the rectory, only to find that I had locked myself out! "Ohmygod!"

Next door to the rectory there is a Gulf Oil station. I sprinted over to the pay phone there, only to discover that I had no change in my pockets. Neither did the lone attendant; so I sat down by one of the gas pumps and waited for a customer with a nickel. The attendant looked at his watch.

"Must be a mighty important phone call, Reverend."

"Yes. You see, I went out to use the police radio in my car, forgot the door key, got locked out; so I've got to wake up my assistant, who's asleep upstairs, so that he can come down and let me in, so that I can get my coat and collar and then go out to Diamond Road, so that—"

He was looking at me with wide, wide eyes.

19

All of a sudden I realized how very funny it must have sounded. And sitting there by the gas pump, I doubled up in fits of convulsive laughter. The attendant scratched his head and for a long time stared hard at the new priest who laughed a lot.

A motorist finally drove in, and I borrowed the needed nickel and awakened a perplexed Father Mokarzel who let me in.

Soon I was properly clerically clad and was back on Channel C, talking with my newfound dispatcher friend, Henry—who must have wondered where the hell I had been. Then began a series of patient directions, until I finally reached Chef Menteur Highway.

"Okay, Padre—you've got it made. Now just keep going till you hit Downman Road, turn left, and watch for 1181 Levee—O.K.?"

"10-04—and thank you. Thank you very much."

So I began to drive slowly along the busy highway, pausing at each street, shining my car's police spotlight on each street sign, looking for Diamond Road. I was determined not to call in again and sound like a lost tourist—or worse. So I kept going—and going—and going.

I drove for miles, slowing down at each street, getting farther and farther out into the country. I was thinking again about the urgent death message that I was supposed to deliver, when the sickening thought finally hit me: God, I'm lost!

I remembered that just yesterday on Channel A, I had heard the code letter GOA (Gone on Arrival). I had thought that they were saying DOA (Dead on Arrival) and sped to the given location, only to find nothing. Could I have misunderstood the dispatcher tonight?

With the lights of the city far behind me, I decided to swallow any pride that I might have left and nervously picked up the radio mike once again and said, in a very small voice, "Car 30 to Channel C."

There was a long pause. "Come in, 30."

"I hate to tell you this, but I think I'm lost again. In fact, I think I'm entering Mississsippi!"

There was another long pause. Could he be laughing—or falling off his chair? Dispatchers on the "Adam 12" TV show didn't laugh.

Henry, who was definitely going to be nominated for sainthood by me first thing in the morning, finally coughed a bit and said softly, "Where are you, Father?"

"Well, there's a big plant on the right—it looks like a huge factory."

Henry's cool, impassive voice coached, "That's Michoud. The missile site. What you want to do is turn around 180 degrees and go back on the same highway that you came out. You'll find Downman Road about thirty miles back on your right."

I took a deep breath. "Can I ask you one more thing that might sound very stupid?"

"10-04. Go ahead."

"How—how do *you* spell 'Diamond'?"

I was sure that there must have been a hundred police cars on the streets of New Orleans at that moment, and in my mind I pictured every one of them with two policemen who were holding their stomachs, howling in gales of laughter, screaming at the new chaplain's foolish question, "How do you spell 'Diamond'?"

But I *had* to know.

"I spell it D-O-W-N-M-A-N—how do *you* spell it?"

"I was spelling it D-I-A-M-O-N-D. I thought you had said 'Diamond.'"

"No problem, sir—and you know what?—it's *good* to have you with us!"

It was my turn to smile and relax. "That's 10-04 for me, too. And I'm going to brush up—fast—on my New Orleans accent!"

CHAPTER 4

Bunko on Bourbon Street

12:00 MIDNIGHT

THE MEN SLOUCHED like three pieces of old, tattered rope on a bench in Lafayette Square. They were three of the legion of derelicts who live in a section of New Orleans on or near Camp Street—the street of broken lives and busted dreams; the street occupied by men and women who have long ago given up; the street of cheap wine, rotgut alcohol, and drugs.

Every city in the world has its Skid Row—and New Orleans is no exception. Social experts believe that there are about seven hundred denizens in this ten-square-block area: poor, helpless, vacant-eyed human beings, some of whom at one time were successful lawyers, priests, businessmen, bankers, realtors, ministers, farmers, jockies. They live in squalid, filthy, tiny rooms and sleep on piles of soiled clothes or broken-down beds when sleep finally does close their eyes on another miserable, booze-shrouded day. One of the few rays of hope in their lives is a free meal every afternoon at 4:15 at Ozanam Inn, run by the Brothers of the Good Shepherd, or at the Baptist Mission or the Salvation Army Lodge.

Men begin lining up at Ozanam at 3:00 in the afternoon and are inspected by an eagle-eyed Brother. If they are visibly drunk or are on drugs, they don't pass. There is room for fifty transients to get a shower, a meal, and a night's sleep in a clean bed at the Inn, but their stay is limited to four days; the philosophy is that after four days a man should be able to find work and start supporting himself—or move on. Most of them, however, do not *want* to work; most just exist day by day, night by night, begging a drink or sharing a bottle of "dago red" with two or three of their buddies of the moment.

Camp Street can also be an area of violence. Blood flows almost as freely as the brain-boggling booze. Fights erupt with breathtaking suddenness and end as quickly—fights over such topics as who took the largest gulp from the now-empty bottle, or how old the bartender is, or whether or not One-Eyed Smitty is sleeping with his alcoholic landlady. Some of the goriest scenes take place in the back alleys of Camp Street.

I remember the night that a Latin from South America and his woman were caught together in his flophouse by her common-law husband. They were beaten senseless by four of the husband's friends and were carried off and left lying together—nude and bloody—in a parking lot on Camp Street.

Another time, a jagged wine bottle severed the neck artery of a drunken man. He bled to death while his two friends sat by finishing the pint. As they gulped the last of the "Christmas trees" (pills) and swigged the booze, they watched with unbelieving, bleary eyes as their friend quietly died.

During the day, many of the habitués of Camp Street branch out to conduct business in other areas of the city. One of their favorite targets is a church—Catholic, Jewish, Methodist, Baptist, Moslem; it doesn't really make any difference. Their network, their radar system, is uncanny; word spreads faster than the speed of sound. Some mysterious gyro tells them where a new or young priest or minister resides. Details are shared: what is the best time to approach him; what not to say; and, what is *most* undesirable, those places where *work* is the price of a meal ticket or a handout.

23

The three unshaven, heavy-lidded men on the bench in Lafayette Square were passing around a new bit of information. The leader put down yesterday's *States-Item* newspaper and said, "O.K. Murph, you're the one that's going, ya hear? Me and Bill wuz there on Tuesday. Now get it straight: make sure you get the old man—the one that always wears a black beanie on his head; don't get the younger guy! If you do, you're outta luck! He'll try to put ya to work! The old man with the beanie hands out little envelopes without even talkin' to ya or givin' free advice. And there's a deuce in every envelope!"

And so, Murph, armed with this data, headed for Our Lady of Guadalupe Church and the old man wearing the black beanie.

Later that evening, mission accomplished, and fortified with three bottles of cheap red, they soddenly fell asleep near the Square. Murph's head hung over the curb, perilously close to the rear tire of a parked car. Tomorrow, they dream, could be another great day.

Pastors, priests, ministers, and rabbis, especially those in inner-city parishes, face a monumental problem of how to handle the begging calls at their rectory door. Are they genuine or phony? The eternal debate rages: "He who gives a cup of water in My name—" versus "He's going to buy more death-dealing liquor or pills with what I give him."

Each parish and synagogue usually has a group that handles the poor and the needy who live within their parish confines. In a sympathetic, dignified, and efficient manner, the St. Vincent de Paul Society, for example, is one of the many groups of dedicated laymen who diagnose whether the person's need is real or fictitious and determine how much help—whether money, food, medicine, or furniture—is needed. Then a follow-up by the pastor or his assistant is arranged.

In our parish, Richard Keithley and our St. Vincent de

Paul group do a fine job aiding the most needy cases in the Iberville Housing Project. Along with this organization, other similar groups perform a valiant and vital job—aiding the poor—with little or no help from the general public.

But in every parish, especially in a busy, downtown area, the eternal problem is always present: how to handle the itinerant; the professional panhandler; the man who claims he is hungry—"Just enough for a bowl of soup or some red beans, Father. I swear to you on my First Communion Day!"

What to do?

Some pastors have an unequivocal and flat "No deal!" with these poor unfortunate alcoholics, addicts, or bums. Some give five-minute sermonettes on the evils of drink. Some offer them work for a couple of hours around the church grounds. Others come up with a buck and say, "God bless you. Now beat it!" But most dig down in their own pockets and give some kind of temporary help.

There are many ladies and gentlemen on Camp Street today who are willing to testify, however, that priests and ministers are still the biggest and easiest "hits"—real live patsies.

When I first came to New Orleans I used to wonder why the tremendous number of callers arrived at the rectory on Monday morning, all claiming, "Just got out of jail, Father—I've got to get to Mobile (or Houston or Natchez) by tonight. Can you help me?" I later found out that one of the friendly police officers at CLU (Central Lockup) was telling the men as he let them out, "Drop by and see the priest at Saint Jude's. He'll take care of you!"

The systems and schemes that swindlers and con men use to outwit and out-pocketbook priests and ministers in churches are almost unbelievable. They *have* tried, *are* trying, and *will* try every and any trick in the book.

The slickest con that I ever encountered was a classic—a real work of art.

It was about twelve midnight, and with evening newspaper in hand, I was about to retire. There had been a number of emergency calls that day; a tough marriage counselling session; two masses; a pile of mail that finally got answered; and a meeting of the League of St. Jude in the evening. It had been a long and draining day. And I was *tired.*

The phone rang sharply and a voice, with bar sounds and music in the background, inquired, "Are you Reverend Peter Rogers?"

"Yes, I am."

"My name is Henry Gelpe. I'm the bartender at the 400 Club on Bourbon Street. I wonder if you could help us out?"

The 400 Club was a strip joint on "The Street." Gentlemen from Indianapolis or Fort Worth or Sandusky, usually here on convention or business, would wander down there, following a satisfying New Orleans meal at one of the fine restaurants. Walking The Street they would hear the enticing music, get a quick look inside the dimly lit sex shops, and usually fall victim to the lure of the doorman's pitch which promised untold joys that would "never be forgotten."

That was the 400 Club.

"If I can, Mr. Gelpe. What's the problem?"

"I've got a young man working for me here as a dishwasher. He's a Mexican boy from California, and he's doing so good that in a few weeks I'm going to promote him to assistant barkeep. His name is Ricardo Besan."

I waited.

"See, I received this telegram about an hour ago from Ricardo's brother that his mother had been killed in a car accident near San Jose in California—and his sister was in the car, too, and is dying in the hospital out there. The family wants Ricardo to come home before she dies. Those of us who work here at the club have gotten together, and we took up a collection to help pay his way out there. But—" The man paused and swallowed hard. "He's such a nice guy that no one here wants to tell him. And that's what we're asking, Father, that *you* tell him; that you break the news about his mother and sister."

"O.K. But why me?"

"Because he says, being Mexican, he goes to your church now and then—the church of Our Lady of Guadalupe. You might have seen him there."

I looked at my watch. It was ten past twelve. "All right, Mr. Gelpe. Tell him to come by. I'll meet him at the front door of the rectory in ten minutes."

"Thanks, Padre—you're great! No money, remember—just break the news."

Fifteen minutes later the bell rang and a tall Latin stood there. "Father Rogers?" he began. "My name is Ricardo."

"Come in. How are you doing?"

"Fine—but—" Surprise and curiosity filled his face. "Why did you send for me? Why did Henry let me off work early?"

Gently I led him inside and headed with him to the kitchen. "How about a beer or something to drink, Ricardo?"

The man took a beer; I poured a Coke. Very softly, sitting across from him at the kitchen table, I began a narration on what this world is all about; why man was created in the first place; and that heaven is really our permanent residence. I then led him into some thoughts on the mystery of suffering, the "why" of it all, and that as Christians we must be ready to accept our cross, whatever it might be. And then, as gently as I could, I told him that there had been an accident in California and that his brother had sent a telegram saying that his mother had been killed—and his sister badly hurt.

There was a loud shriek; the man's face twisted in a horrible grief mask, and he fell on his knees by the kitchen table. "*OHHHH, nooooo—Madre mia—mi vida—mi cora-zon!*" His moaning was followed by loud, racking sobs; it seemed that the man's very existence was being snuffed out by grief and sorrow and misery and loss.

After a few moments he tried to regain his composure and sat at the table with his head in his brown, calloused hands. Then looking directly into my eyes he whispered, "She was so proud when I served as *monaguillo*—an altar boy—in *mi parroquia* in California." Tears flooded his eyes as he continued. "I used to sing in the choir, too—church of Santa Teresa in San Jose." He put his face on his arms, and his body again was racked with heaving sobs.

His dark brown eyes looked up again. "So that's why they gave me this money—and no one at the place I worked said a word." He fished out $23.00 in ones and fives and some change.

"Now I see. They were trying to pay my way home—to bury my mother."

"Twenty-three dollars? Is that all you've got?"

"That's all. But I was going to get a raise in a couple of weeks."

I went to the phone and dialed the Greyhound Bus Station. I was told that the bus fare to San Francisco was $75.00—one way.

"When would that bus arrive in San Francisco?" I asked the clerk.

I was told that it would take fifty-two hours and that the next bus didn't leave till 6:30 in the morning!

Putting down the phone, I turned again to the man who was now quietly staring with unseeing eyes at the beer bottle's label. Tears were streaming down his face, but he didn't make a sound. I looked at him intently for a long moment.

Picking up the phone again, I dialed National Airlines. They told me that the air fare to San Francisco, round-trip, was $350 and that there was a night flight departing from

New Orleans at 2:10—arriving there at 6:45 A.M., California time. I made a reservation, saying that the ticket would be picked up at the airport before the flight.

"Ricardo," I explained, "if you took a bus in the morning, you'd never get there in time for your mother's funeral. So I'm going to lend you the money to fly out there. In a week or two, when you return and get back your job, you can repay me. I'll call Mr. Gelpe tomorrow at the 400 Club."

A look of disbelief and gratitude crossed the man's face. "*Ay, Padre–que hermoso; usted es muy amable.*" And he tried to kiss my hand.

"We've got to hurry, friend. It's almost one o'clock now; you've only got an hour to get packed and get out to the airport. Do you have another suit?"

The man looked down at his Levis and faded shirt. "No, I arrived here with very little. But I will be saving for—"

"O.K. Look, Ricardo, I believe you. And I feel sorry for you, and I'm going to help you. I'm going to loan you four hundred dollars. We'll buy a round-trip ticket at the airport, and you get yourself an inexpensive suit when you arrive out there."

"Padre, you are so good—but you don't have to drive me to the airport. I shall take a city bus out there."

"No time, Ricardo. Let's get moving."

And as Ricardo embraced me with a brotherly *abrazo*, tears streamed down his brown, leathery face.

"Can we pass by the 400 Club?" the man timidly asked as we rose. "I have a locker there where I change. I'll pick up a few little things."

"Sure, but just for a minute, Ricardo. *Un minuto; entiende?*"

While Ricardo went to the bathroom to wash up, I slipped into my office and took down the *National Catholic Directory* from the shelf; this is the book that contains every Catholic parish in every diocese and archdiocese in the United States. I quickly flipped to the archdiocese of San Francisco, found San Jose, and ran my finger down the list of churches there. Sure enough, there it was— Santa Teresa parish, Cahalan and Calero streets, San Jose, California.

Feeling a bit guilty about doubting the grief-stricken man, I went to the church safe and withdrew four hundred dollars in cash, marking the petty cash slip "charity," giving the man's name, date, etc. I was sure that the airlines would not accept a check, especially one given by Ricardo. As I slipped the money into the distraught man's hand, I gently put my arm on his back and said, "O.K., Ricardo, let's go."

The Cobra slid around the few blocks to Bourbon Street, which was alive and noisy as always, and came to a halt at the 400 Club when Ricardo said, "Please let me out by that green side-door, Padre. That's the employee's entrance. Wait for me, *Padrecito,* I'll only be a minute—only a minute." And he disappeared into the green side-door.

Fifteen minutes later, my motor was still running, and I was watching every time the employee's green side-door would open. I was becoming impatient. *Tiempo Mexicano,* I thought, looking at my watch. I figured that the poor devil was busy saying good-bye to Henry and the employees and friends inside, telling them that he was *flying* out there!

Ten minutes later, a tough-looking stripper with flaming red hair and a low low-cut gown came out, and I stopped her. "Pardon me; I'm Father Rogers and I was wondering if Ricardo is ready yet? We've got to hurry to make it to the airport."

She looked me up and down, moved the gum to the other side of her mouth, and said, "Ricardo? I don't know no Ricardo." And she jumped into a waiting cab for more important tasks.

In two seconds I was inside the green side-door. No Ricardo Besan—no Mexican boy ever worked there. There was no bartender named Henry Gelpe, and no telegram about a death notice had arrived that night!

A tired-looking waitress came over and said that she had seen a Mexican-type man enter through the employee's entrance—almost knocked her over, in fact—about twenty minutes ago. But he headed right out the front door. "And I didn't see no tears or sadness on his face," she added.

"I guess *not!*" I muttered.

As I slowly walked back to the car, realizing that I had been taken, I heard a Dixieland jazz trumpet's "wa-wa-wa" coming from a nearby club. Was it a taunt? No, I thought grimly. It wasn't a taunt. It was more like a sad dirge. A dirge because a man had lied on his mother's death for a few lousy dollars.

Three weeks later I was attending the monthly District Clergy Conference at Corpus Christi Church on St. Bernard Avenue. Following the meeting, the usual clerical chitchat took place over a couple of cocktails before lunch was served. Idly swishing a martini, I joined one group of priests as Fr. Tom Kelly, one of our Oblates, was saying, "And I thought something was wrong with the call—just a hunch—so I told the guy to wait till morning, and I'd tell him then."

"Tom, what was that?" I asked.

"Last night I got this weird call from a guy who said he was a headwaiter at The Court of the Two Sisters. He claimed that his busboy's father had just been killed in California. They had taken up a collection for him to get out there, but no one wanted to break the news to him, and would I—"

"Yeah, yeah—I know! Want to bet I know the name of that poor 'busboy?' Ten to one it was Ricardo Besan!"

"It sure was, Pete. Don't tell me he got to *you?*"

Ricardo Besan and his friend are in prison today because they were too greedy. He and his partner had pulled that same stunt on priests and ministers throughout New Mexico and Texas and were in the process of sweeping up Louisiana. Very few of the clergy reported the rip-off to the police; there were just a couple of complaints on record. Perhaps the men of the cloth were too ashamed that they had been victims of such a hoax, or perhaps they did not want to face a man who would swear and lie on his mother's name.

Every parish in the archdiocese of New Orleans receives a weekly résumé of news, reports of seminars, CCD meetings, and goings-on. It is called the *Clergy Bulletin*. A few day later, after hearing that Ricardo Besan had not only hit Guadalupe, but also St. Monica's, and had attempted to hit the cathedral, I decided that he might try again. So I typed up a description of the man and his usual MO and how to handle it if he phoned any other parish or convent in the archdiocese.

Two months later a priest at St. John the Baptist parish read my account of the con artist in the *Clergy Bulletin*. Soon after, he received a call, late at night, this time from the "manager" of Broussard's Restaurant. Following instructions, the priest told the man to drop around to St. John's rectory in a half hour. He would, sadly and reluctantly, break the terrible news to Ricardo that his mother had been killed. Perhaps the poor grieving son could even use a few dollars.

The police were notified, and two detectives from the Bunko Squad positioned themselves in the next room while the good Padre handed over three hundred dollars so that the distraught "son" could get out to California as fast as possible to attend his mother's funeral.

In a moment, the con man's sick and slick game came to an abrupt, grinding halt as handcuffs snared his greedy hands—the hands of a man who swore and lied on his mother's death for a few lousy dollars.

CHAPTER 5

They Called Him "Jimmy"

11:05 A.M.

IT WAS SUNDAY, January 7, 1973. A light mist ushered in the saddest day in the history of the New Orleans Police Department.

I was scheduled to celebrate the 11:30 Sunday mass at Our Lady of Guadalupe, and since confessions are heard fifteen minutes before each service, I was getting ready to go over to the church. At 11:05 the phone rang and a voice screamed, "Father—the Howard Johnson Motel is on fire. I'm in a drugstore nearby. I think a fireman just fell off a ladder."

And so began twenty-eight hours of sheer hell; twenty-eight hours during which the entire police department—and fire department—were held at bay by an apparently crazed gunman named Mark Essex. The whole nation—the whole world—watched in stunned disbelief as the young black man ran from window to window, from floor to floor, in the posh downtown motel, setting fires to the furnishings in the rooms and firing with uncanny and deadly precision at men in uniform below.

Sgt. Emmanuel Palmisano and three of the men from the First were cautiously peering around the corner of the DeMontluzin Building on the Gravier Street side, when I arrived. Police and sheriff's department cars had surrounded the hotel, and shots were sporadically ringing out. I moved in behind an officer who had his rifle trained up at the swimming pool area on the eighth floor. I poked my head around one of the policemen and, looking up, was able to get a fleeting look at a young man with a medium Afro, before he ducked behind some potted plants along the wall of the swimming pool.

"Get back, Chaplain!" one of the men shouted sharply behind me. "He don't miss!" He continued, "A fireman was going up the ladder to get to the fire when some bastard shot him right off it! I don't know if he's dead or not; they just took him to Charity."

Charity Hospital's emergency ramp is located just about two blocks from the front of the motel. "I'll run over and see him," I said. "Is the chief here?"

"He's setting up a command post in the lobby of the motel. I understand they're calling in a lot of our people. We don't know how many snipers are up there."

I decided then to check with Chief Clarence Giarrusso. Giarrusso, who also has a law degree, is a career policeman who served as captain in the Narcotics Squad before being named chief in 1971. Like his brother Joe before him, Giarrusso was doing a fine job as boss of the 1,200-strong New Orleans Police Department. He was a no-nonsense, tough cop—but had a heart for his men. I recalled that just eight days before, a young black police cadet named Alfred Harrell had been killed by a mysterious sniper who had shot a .44 magnum into the driveway at Central Lockup. On that night, as I finished giving the Last Blessing to the dead cadet in Charity Hospital's emergency room, I looked up and saw the chief with head bowed—tears unashamedly streaming down his lined face.

Without a word to anyone, I decided to find the chief that morning. I took off suddenly, running with all speed possible across the street toward the lobby of the motel. I dashed across the open street, which all of a sudden seemed two miles wide, in a crouching position. Just after reaching the sidewalk, a powerful set of arms grabbed me and pulled me against the wall of the motel.

"You crazy, Padre?"

I looked up into the face of Chief Giarrusso. "Hi, Chief. Just wanted to tell you good morning." I grinned.

But the chief wasn't smiling.

Inside the lobby an array of desks, telephones, and two-way radios was being set up. Men, in uniform and out of uniform, were arriving to make war on an apparently demented murderer—or murderers. Chief Louis Sirgo, the Number Two man in the department, was listening to a team of police. Sirgo had left a nice job in civilian life at the invitation of Chief Giarrusso to help in the administration of the complex department. He was well liked; a real family man—and a cool cop.

Chief Louis Turner, Number Three man on the force, next entered the lobby in a running crouch. A gentle black man with a sense of humor, he had been promoted from the ranks—from Auto Pound to Urban Squad to Districts to the third-ranking spot in the department.

And the question on his and everyone's mind was: "What the hell is happening here?"

What no one knew was that, at that very moment upstairs, the killer had been surprised, as he was setting fire to another room and the corridor carpet outside room 1815, by a young doctor, Robert V. Stegall. He then put his .44 magnum to the doctor's head and cooly blew his head open. Elizabeth Stegall, the doctor's young wife, screamed and ran to her dying husband. As she sobbed and cradled her man's bloody head on her breast; the killer (or an accomplice) came up behind her and at close range drilled a shot into her head. The young couple, when officers found them later, were locked in a grisly death embrace. A red, green, and black flag, the emblem of the African Liberation Army, was spread near the bodies.

Downstairs, at Command Headquarters, Turner faced

the chief. "Charley Arnold's been hit. He's on the ninth floor of the building across the street." He listened again, then added, "Charley got it in the face!"

Clutching the little black kit that contained the holy oils, I raced back across the street before anyone knew I was gone. Other feet pounded behind me. We made it to the shelter of the DeMontluzin Building again and headed for the elevators. Nine floors up I found a group of officers crouching at the sides of office windows, rifles and pistols in their hands. Their buddy, Charley Arnold, lay on the floor, holding his face. He was moaning low and twisting over and over.

"Lay still, Charley," I told him as I put my handkerchief to the smashed portion of what used to be the left side of his jaw. "Let's get out of here. . . . Can you walk?"

Maj. Tony Duke and a few others helped lift the wounded officer to his feet. I was whispering softly in the man's ear as I held the cloth to his face. "Say after me, 'O my God, I am heartily sorry—'" and through blood and bits of teeth, Arnold wheezed those words of contrition to his Saviour as we headed down to a waiting emergency unit.

I turned to Duke. "O.K. if I ride with him? There's a fireman over at the hospital too." And for the two-block ride to the hospital a wounded soldier, to the music of a screaming siren, prayed for his life.

The scene at Charity Hospital's emergency room was grim. Charity is used to blood and violence and accidents. The vast hospital, second largest in the nation, handles over 375,000 cases every year; of these, most are accidents, shootings, stabbings, and other forms of violence. The emergency section of this huge monolith is a unit that defies classification, a depository where the crippled, the scarred, the most painful cases come after they have lost and "the streets have won again." Charity, at that time with young and capable Dr. Charles Mary as its director, is one of the most active city hospitals in the United States. Interns and doctors from all over the world come to soak up the experience and expertise that this busy hospital can offer.

On that fateful day in January, all systems were on red alert. Extra doctors and nurses were called in; workmen were busy boarding up windows that fronted the Howard Johnson Motel side. (A few shots had been fired from the motel toward the hospital.) Charity had been transformed into a battlefield station for those twenty-eight hours. Wounded and dead policemen and civilians were brought in—victims of a senseless bloodbath. Radio and TV stations were pleading for blood donors throughout the day and night.

When they lifted Officer Arnold from the unit and sped him to the emergency room, I went looking for the wounded firefighter.

"He's Lieutenant Tim Ursin," a fireman in his company told me. "He was shot in the arm as he climbed the ladder. He was the first one up and that son-of-a-bitch—'scuse me, Father—waited for him and then let him have it! He's in surgery now. The last word from one of the docs is that he might lose his arm."

I grasped the man's arm tightly in silent salute and went to look for Tim's wife, Mary, who had been doing the laundry when notified that her husband was injured. She had rushed out of the house leaving her little boy, Timmy, Jr., with a neighbor. Now she was bewildered and perplexed as she sought out the chaplain.

"I hear he might lose his arm." It was more of a question than a statement.

"No, honey," I told her. "Maybe a finger or two, but they're working like crazy to save the arm."

The young wife, eyes wide with fear, dabbed at tears

with a Kleenex and turned away. "And to think I didn't want him to become a policeman; I thought it was too dangerous!"

A cop walked by with a portable radio, and I asked, "How's it going over there?"

"Bad, Padre—bad. The nut is running from floor to floor; I hear he's killed a young honeymoon couple that he found in one of the rooms. Apparently he's got a passkey to all the rooms. One guest, a guy named Ed Frasier, has been playing possum on the porch outside his room for the past four hours, pretending he's dead, afraid to move." The veteran police officer shook his head in disbelief. "I've been on this job for sixteen years. I never saw *anything* like this!"

"I'll be going back over there. If you need me here, I'll be on Channel 3—O.K.?"

I went out through the emergency ramp, radio in my back pocket, and began the two-and-a-half-block walk back to the motel. The street was in the direct line of fire, and as I walked by the Warwick Hotel, a block away, I saw a tourist standing in the middle of the street, laden with cameras, looking at a map. She was completely oblivious to all the danger and commotion. I caught up with her and said, "Ma'am, you'd better get back to the shelter of that hotel. There's a maniac loose shooting at anything that he—or they—can see, and I—"

"Just a minute, Preacher," the woman snapped. "I've saved for five years to come to New Orleans—'the city that care forgot,' the Chamber of Commerce booklet said. I've got two more days here, and you're trying to tell me to get off the streets. Why—"

At that moment another volley of shots was heard not too far away. I very firmly escorted the unwilling tourist to the shelter of the Warwick Hotel lobby. The infuriated woman, still not realizing the danger, began berating me, and as I walked away, she called out, "I'm going to report you to someone. Who is your superior?"

Moving back toward the Howard Johnson, I smiled back at the woman and said, "Pope Paul the Sixth!"

Directly in front of the Howard Johnson Motel is a small park-area called Duncan Plaza. The Louisiana State Supreme Court and the State Office Building are behind the Plaza; City Hall is to the left of the motel and the New Orleans Public Library's main branch is to the right.

A number of police cars were lined up at the edge of the Plaza, forming a kind of semicircle barricade against the sniper. Like wagon trains in a Western, I thought. Sgt. Emmanuel "Pal" Palmisano, a thirteen-year veteran, was crouched behind his car, 130, reloading his rifle. He spotted the chaplain running toward him.

"Keep down, Father," Pal advised. "He's on the ninth floor now, right above us, and he's been shooting this way."

After a few moments of chatter with him I said, "Take care, Pal," and dashed about twenty yards to the hook and ladder fire truck located to the left of Car 130. A group of firefighters were crouching behind the machine, all peering up intently. These men were used to fighting fires, not people.

"How's Ursin, Padre?" Fire Capt. Wally Bailey asked.

"They're working on him now. There's a chance he might lose his arm."

Bailey was off duty at the time but volunteered his services when he heard about the sniper. Suddenly a burst of fire erupted again, Automatically, the entire group ducked down, and a young firefighter who had recently returned from Vietnam whispered to no one in particular, "God, we did this over there—but what the hell is happening here?"

Suddenly John Coggins, a fireman for over thirty years,

stood up and shouted, "They got that policeman!" And he pointed to Sgt. Pal Palmisano lying near Car 130.

In a matter of seconds, Bailey, myself, and one or two others were at the sergeant's side. He lay on the ground, his loaded gun a few feet away. His face was contorted with pain as he held his left shoulder. A policeman grabbed Palmisano's car radio and called for a unit. Bailey snatched the sergeant's rifle and, crouching behind the police car, covered us.

After what seemed an eternity, the police unit wheeled alongside. Chris Caton, the driver (who was later wounded), and I lifted the bleeding man onto the stretcher. When Palmisano was secure on the stretcher, two of the officers lifted him as quickly as possible into the open ambulance doors. More shots were heard over to the left.

I was picking up my sick-call kit from the ground when a dull, sickening *thud* dug into the grass not more than three feet away from me. It was one .44 magnum slug that missed. I yanked open the front door of the ambulance and literally dove into the seat. Chris was closing the back doors when I glanced back to the left.

My blood froze at what I saw.

Lying close to a large tree, about twenty feet away, was a young policeman. The glazed look of death already masked his face. Officer Ken Solis, also badly wounded, was attempting to crawl over to help his comrade. The wounded cop put his bloodied hand on the man's chest, then dropped his head in grief and hopelessness.

"It's Phil Coleman," the driver grimly said. "I'll come back for him. Hold on."

As the emergency unit took off for Charity's ramp, the back doors flew open and the stretcher, with a bleeding Palmisano on it, almost slid out. Reaching back quickly, I grabbed the stretcher and held it for the fastest ride in history to the hospital, whispering words of prayer and comfort in Palmisano's ear.

I was in the emergency room with Palmisano when they brought in the dead Officer Coleman and his wounded friend, Ken Solis. As I pulled down the sheet from the young officer's bloody face and administered the last rites *sub conditione,* a motorcycle man, standing nearby slowly muttered, "Son of a bitch—who's going to tell Pat?" Later I found out that Pat was Coleman's wife and that he had a little boy who had been sick.

And so, on that dreadful afternoon on which a hate-filled man or men wreaked vengeance on other human beings, I was phoning a young widow to come down to Charity and meet me. "Yes, your husband has been hit—I'll explain everything when I see you. And I hope your little boy is feeling better."

Back at the Howard Johnson Motel, the scene was worsening. A terrified motel maid was relating to the police how the killer suddenly confronted her in the room in which she was hiding.

"He pointed that big gun at me and laughed," she recalled. The young black girl was trembling violently as she added, "All of a sudden a white man came out of the next room and got between me and the man with the gun—like to protect me."

"Go on, honey," Chief Sirgo urged.

"Well, when the dude saw that, he told the white boy, 'Fella—you just saved your life and you saved that black chick's life, too.' And then he ran up the stairs fast—very fast." And she began sobbing.

New Orleans police, state police, sheriff's deputies, Jefferson Parish police, the FBI—all were working. The motel is surrounded by tall buildings, including the Rault Center, which had just a few weeks previously suffered a tragic high-rise fire. On each of the buildings, police sharpshooters were positioned with high-powered rifles. All watched intently for a sign of a young man—or men— who apparently had made a pact with death in this attempt to destroy authority—especially authority wearing a uniform.

Giarrusso and his men at the Command Desk in the lobby were talking, discussing, planning, determining locations, listening to witnesses.

"He's hit a man by the swimming pool. The man, a Robert Bemish, we believe, is floating in the pool. Don't know if he's dead or what," reported one of the men listening to Channel 3.

"Is the gunman there now?" snapped the chief.

"No, he's gone. They think he went up the south stairwell right now—about the eleventh floor."

As in any battle that ever was fought, rumors were flying like bits of straw in a hurricane. One of the rumors making the rounds with civilians was that the Rault Center fire, which had damaged the top stories, had been deliberately set by the killer just weeks ago so that no police officers would be able to use that location to fire down on him at the Howard Johnson Motel just across the street. Other rumors circulating were that certain policemen were killed or missing. Then after a while one of the officers mentioned would suddenly appear from some position or other.

The word was *confusion*.

Maids, motel guests, and motel personnel who were able to slip down the stairwells were being stopped and identified and questioned by the police before they were permitted to leave. Rumors then began that the killer's accomplices had dressed as maids and janitors and had escaped with the regular motel employees.

It was an unbelievable afternoon and evening, and as the clock ticked on, millions of people stopped their work, stopped their play, stopped their schoolwork, stopped whatever they were doing all over the world, and sat down in utter and total anguish as they watched an army rendered powerless.

It was not known at that time by the Command Desk in the lobby, but both the manager and assistant manager, who earlier in the day had gone up to investigate the report of fires being set, would never walk down the stairs of their hotel again.

Fifty-two-year-old Frank Schneider, the assistant manager, had first gone up to the eleventh floor to check the fire report. The murderer met him there and killed him with two .44 magnum rifle shots. Later, Walter Collins, the affable manager of the Howard Johnson, went to see what had kept Schneider so long. Tragically, he found out.

He ran into the killer—or killers—on the tenth floor and was hit by a .44 magnum slug in the stomach and fell in the stairwell. When police were finally able to get to him, he was still alive but mortally wounded. He was rushed to Charity Hospital where he clung to life for eight days before dying in his wife's arms on January 15, 1973.

Paul Persigo was a young cop who was popular with everyone. At thirty-three he was proud of a good record, having served the people of New Orleans as a policeman for five years. He was even more proud of his sweet wife Judy and his three young children: Mark, ten; Steven, eight; and Holly, three.

Paul was worried about little Holly; her tiny legs were not growing straight and normal. So she had spent most of the time in a specially made, stirruplike brace which was supposed to correct the trouble. She looked almost pathetic, for she walked with a peculiar kind of hobble. Doctors assured Paul and Judy, however, that it would only be for a few months—or maybe a year.

"And then I'll race you to the store for a Snow Cone," Paul would tell her.

"But I can't *run,* Daddy," Holly would say.

"Don't worry about that—I'm gonna teach you how; 'cause I'm the best runner in the world!" And they both would laugh. And he would hold her high and hug her.

They got to Paul Persigo's body—he had been shot in the mouth and stilled in death by a .44 magnum bullet —shortly after Phil Coleman had been killed in Duncan Plaza. Neither of his three little children would ever see their daddy's face again. There would never be a race with Holly for a Snow Cone. A senseless murder robbed the world of another good father—and another good policeman.

"Where the *hell* is the elevator? It's been up on eighteen for a damn long time!" A man from the Tack Squad muttered.

Word soon came from Command Desk that it looked like two policemen were trapped in the elevator which had mysteriously stalled on the top floor.

"Those two men are sitting ducks. They can be shot through the elevator doors," Chief Louis Sirgo observed. That's when he decided to take a number of volunteers and use the stairs to get to the two officers caged in the stalled car.

Giarrusso didn't like the idea; but Sirgo, in his quiet, offhand way, chuckled. "Probably it's just stuck from all that heat from the fires on those floors. Those men must feel like barbequed hamburger at an FOP picnic by now. I think we'd better go up."

44

It was not known to anyone at that moment, as Chief Sirgo and his volunteers cautiously began to climb the eighteen stories on their mission of rescue, that the Howard Johnson tragedy did not really begin on Sunday, January 7, 1973. The whole terrible affair had begun exactly one hour before the new year arrived, one week ago.

Subsequent police work and anonymous tips unearthed a bizarre tale of a young man, either alone or with help, who carved a bloody and erratic trail that wound through the streets of New Orleans and eventually terminated in a pool of blood from his riddled body on the roof of the Howard Johnson Motel.

One week previous, according to the official police report, at 10:55 P.M. on New Year's Eve, Mark Essex had positioned himself in a vacant lot adjacent to Perdido Street, to the rear of the New Orleans Police Headquarters. He had parked his car, a '63 blue Chevy, in the 2800 block of Perdido Street. The car was registered to Essex, and the keys were left in the ignition. When he was in position and sighted police in uniform in the driveway of Central Lockup, he had pumped six rounds of .44 caliber magnum ammunition at them. His joy at hitting two men in uniform must have been short-lived for the man he killed was the young black police cadet, Alfred Harrell. He wounded Lt. Horace Perez, hitting him in the leg and foot in that barrage.

Following the shooting, police history records that he ran across more vacant lots and crossed the I-10 expressway. We can imagine the assassin—stumbling, panting, looking back, as he clutched a lethal .44 rifle, ordered by him from the Montgomery Ward outlet in his hometown of Emporia, Kansas, six months earlier. Along his twisting route were later found a brown leather bag containing two cans of lighter fluid, a sixty-five-foot roll of bell wire, and six live .44 caliber magnum cartridges. Boot prints later lifted from his path determined that it was the same print as Essex's boots.

In that area of town there are many warehouses, some vacant, some occupied. The sniper first grabbed the door handle of the Oliver Van Horn Company at 4100 Euphrosine and began to jerk it violently. Looking around furtively, he fired three shots with his .44 magnum into the lock.

No luck. It wouldn't open.

History follows him as, cursing and swearing, he dashed around the corner and came to the Burkhart Manufacturing Company on 1065 South Gayoso Street. Locked. He checked the doors, the windows, and found an unlocked window.

Inside, he somehow gashed his arm, and blood began to flow. But worse than that, he tripped the ADT alarm system. The silent alarm screamed in a distant post, and the police were alerted. Essex took up a position behind a desk by a window and held his breath as he saw the flashing blue lights of a police car coming toward him.

Sgt. Ed Hosli, a young K-9 officer with four lovely children and a beautiful wife, was the first to arrive; rookie Officer Harold Blappert was with him. In the back seat sat Hosli's pal, partner, and dog, Ike.

Ed was proud to be a member of the K-9 Corps, that unique outfit whose officers have partners who are specially trained dogs. The dogs love their masters and would die for them—and would fearlessly take on the entire Russian army on signal. As Hosli turned back to the car to release Ike, who was already whining, eager to get into combat, a deadly .44 magnum rifle was silently being raised in the darkness of the deep shadows within. Two shots rang out; the young sergeant fell, shot in the back and seriously wounded by the bullets.

Following the shooting of Hosli, the killer was on the run again. He found a little white, wooden Baptist church at 1208 South Lopez Street, about six blocks from the spot where he had shot Sergeant Hosli. He (possibly with friends) must have set track records, for he didn't stop to pick up the ten rounds of .44 magnum cartridges that were later found along his trail.

He broke the front door lock of the tiny church and entered, sleeping and hiding there throughout the night.

Rev. Sylvester Williams, a Baptist preacher, arrived at his little church at 6:00 P.M. on the evening of January 1. He planned to launch the new year in the finest way, with some good old song and prayer at an 8:00 P.M. service. He was about to slip his key into the creaky door when he noticed that the door had been forced open. Entering the tiny temple, he saw a black male in the rear of the church. The reverend hastily darted out and summoned the police. He waited until the police arrived, but when they searched the church, the man had vanished, leaving no trace.

The next evening, Essex again surfaced. At 6:00 P.M., he entered a small neighborhood grocery store named Joe's, located at 4200 Erato Street, where he bought a razor and some blades. Apparently he decided then to return to the church. He hid out there for the next twenty-four hours.

The following day, January 3, at 7:30 P.M., an anonymous caller tipped off the police that a man was again hiding in the church. A short time later, the police were there for the second time, and once again, he was gone. The chase was on.

Essex was gone, but a bag containing some .38 caliber cartridges was found hidden in the bathroom. There was also a note written to the minister of the church apologizing for the break-in. The police crime lab carefully took samples of fresh bloodstains found on benches and on the wall, and later identified them as the same blood type as that of Mark Essex.

From 10:00 P.M. on January 3 until 10:00 A.M. the morning of January 7, there was no trace of the elusive man on the run. Speculation has it that he was hiding in the immediate vicinity, or perhaps he had returned to his apartment, later found to be located on Perdido Street.

All doubt about where he was ended on the morning of January 7, when he again entered Joe's grocery store and shouted, "You come here!"

As the startled grocer looked up, he was gunned down by a bullet from the now infamous .44 caliber magnum. Joe was wounded in the neck and later rushed to the hospital. For months he lived with the possibility of being paralyzed for life, and I visited him at Hotel Dieu Hospital where, although under heavy police protection, he trembled for his life. He alone could identify the assailant.

After shooting Joe the grocer, Essex then ran from the store down to the 1500 block of South White Street, where he spotted Marvin Albert sitting in his car, a blue Ford, with the motor running. At gunpoint, he ordered Albert out and roared off toward Melpomene and Broad streets. Police officer Phil Dominich was on the scene two minutes after Albert's car was stolen.

"Get in," the officer said to Albert.

They careened off in the direction which Essex had taken. They drove up and down the streets, searching the area, but apparently the man had vanished again.

At 10:40 Marvin Albert's stolen car was involved in a hit-and-run accident at Washington Avenue and Dupre Street. As Essex sped away from the scene, the driver of the damaged car copied down the license number of the fleeing vehicle.

At a furious rate of speed, Essex then raced back toward the downtown area.

What thoughts were going through the young man's mind at that moment? Had he *planned* to go to the Howard Johnson Motel? Was he going to meet confederates there? Was it mere chance that, days previously, he had circled in red ink on a map, later found in his apartment, the Howard Johnson Motel? Was all this part of a methodical, well-thought-out master plan or was it just a series of stumbling bits of chance? Chance that was soon to climax in a terrifying and unforgettable ordeal?

The parking attendant at the Howard Johnson's indoor garage couldn't believe his eyes when he saw a blue Ford approaching at such a high rate of speed.

"Slow down!" he shouted, as the young black man sped by him and proceeded up the inside ramp to the fourth floor of the parking garage.

It was now 11:00 A.M. January 7, 1973.

Back at Charity Hospital I was talking to the wives and families of men who had been wounded. The hospital had set up an emergency rest station for them, with coffee, sandwiches, and cold drinks, in the plasma donors' room on the seventh floor. It was a strange sight: people who had never seen each other before—complete strangers just a few hours ago—now bound so closely together by the new but steel-like bonds of mutual tragedy. Each had a loved one fighting for his life.

A nurse called me over and quietly said, "Father, they're looking for you downstairs. They just brought some more in!"

Joe Anderson was an employee of Fire Alarm. It was his job to dispatch fire companies to the location of a fire and to alert all the necessary people. His task, in addition to a thousand other duties, was to order back-up companies to cover for the units that had gone to the fire. When Joe Anderson heard that firefighters were in trouble on that sad

Sunday in January, he hastened to the scene, although he was off duty.

One hour later he was hit by a .44 magnum slug as he crouched near a fire truck not too far from the spot where Paul Persigo had been killed. As I later chatted with the fifty-two-year-old Anderson, who was wounded in the shoulder, they wheeled in the young civilian ambulance driver, Chris Caton, who had been shot in the leg by the now-familiar .44 magnum as he attended the wounded.

Robert Childress had been a New Orleans cop for twelve years. Working out of Auto Pound, he was driving two trustees back to the House of Detention on that disastrous Sunday. When he heard that two people had been shot at the Howard Johnson Motel and that the killer was on the loose, he quickly dropped off his cargo and headed for the scene. He and patrolman Mike Burl, from the First District, were about the first to arrive.

A fireman briefed them on the bizarre happenings: "And the report is that a young couple on their honeymoon were just shot on the eighteenth floor. A fireman up there radioed it in. There's a nut running around with a gun."

"I guess it's you and I," Mike said.

Bob replied, "I guess so. Let's go, Mike!"

They decided that the gunman would probably not be standing around on the eighteenth, so they pushed the buttons on the sixteenth and seventeenth floors. At each floor, Mike, gun in hand, would go out and scout around while Childress held the elevator door open.

They saw no one.

As they ascended higher and higher, the smoke from the burning rooms on the eighteenth got thicker. It seeped into the elevator car.

They reached the eighteenth floor. And the elevator doors wouldn't open.

Suddenly the lights in the elevator went out, the power gone. The phone in the elevator, when they tried to call, was dead. Frantically, they pushed Lobby. They pushed five, nine, eleven—nothing happened.

Bob took out his cigarette lighter, and it flickered for a moment, then went dead.

They banged, pushed, and threw their weight against the stubborn doors. No luck.

"This would be a lousy place to die, wouldn't it?" said Burl.

"Yeah," Bob replied wryly. "Never thought I'd be able to pick out my own coffin, though."

"What are we going to do, Bob?" young Burl asked.

"Let's play it cool, for one thing," advised the veteran police officer.

They put their jackets along the rim of the door, where the smoke was seeping in.

They had been trapped for about an hour when Bob said, "Take off your gun belt. Let's see if we can pry off the top of the car. There must be some kind of emergency hatch."

So, groping, choking, and coughing in the dense smoke, they finally pried open a section from the roof of the car. It was about twenty-two inches square.

"Wanna try it, Mike?" asked Childress. "Go slow, slide down the cables—stop and rest on every floor. Be careful. Eighteen floors is a long way to fall."

"Suppose the power comes on again and the elevator starts down on me?"

"If we get power, I'll keep the elevator up here till you're down."

So Mike Burl climbed out and grasped the greased cables. He left his weapon with Bob, after dropping his gun belt down the long dark shaft as a kind of signal.

"Good luck, partner."

Burl began his slow, torturous descent. At every floor, he shouted back to Bob until his voice became a distant blur. A half hour later, shaken and bruised, with smoke in his lungs and with his hands looking like two pieces of raw meat, he was given oxygen and then sped off to Charity.

"Better go get Childress; I don't know how much longer he can hold out," gasped the injured policeman.

"Chief Sirgo and some men just started up," someone told him. "They should be around the tenth floor by now."

Back in the stalled and dark elevator, Bob again threw his weight against the doors. They suddenly slid back— open!"

The veteran cop could not believe his eyes as he stepped out.

"It looked like something out of a horror movie," he recalls. "Water everywhere—six inches deep. Fixtures hanging loose, bare electric wires, parts of the ceiling out. Smoke pouring up and down the corridor. It was sheer hell."

Gun in hand, Childress cautiously peered into room 1829 where the snorkel was pouring thousands of gallons of water from outside. Hearing noises in 1815, he knocked on the door and identified himself as a police officer.

"Open the door," he commanded.

A muffled voice, filled with fear, responded in the negative.

Childress learned later that two firefighters had barricaded themselves inside the room. They thought he was the gunman. They had not only locked and bolted the door, but had pushed a heavy dresser against it and placed a mattress on top of that. In fear of their lives, they both then lay down on the floor.

Bob next made his way to a balcony and looked down on the swimming pool area. He saw the body of a man floating in the pool, apparently dead, and an elderly couple clutching each other in terror. He spotted Officer Norman Knapp in a building across the street and then realized that there were armed officers in the Rault Center, the DeMontluzin Building, and others. He quickly stepped back inside, but not before noticing the barrel of a rifle—one floor directly below him—aimed at the Rault Center.

As he returned to the foyer in front of the elevators, he saw a pile of debris—with a foot protruding from under it. He pulled off some of the sheet rock and discovered the bodies of the young couple. The woman had been shot once; the man, three times.

Bob checked the pulses of both. There was no doubt that they were dead.

"My God!" he muttered. It was about an hour and a half since he first entered the elevator. Would help *ever* come?

Figuring that the gunman might be using the stairwell, Childress next decided to take the same escape route that Mike Burl did. Praying that the power would not be turned on and that he wouldn't be still another victim of that insane day, he began the long, bloody slide down the steel cables. His descent was agonizingly slow. His arms felt as though there were ton weights tied to each of them.

After what seemed forever, he saw the light from the open doors in the lobby. He staggered into the arms of his fellow officers and choked out a description of the gruesome happenings on the eighteenth. As he was being carried to a waiting unit, a sergeant looked him in the eye.

"That rescue party that went after you fellows—it was led by Chief Louis Sirgo. We just got word that he was killed on the fifteenth floor."

God! When—where—how—would it end?

I had just finished attending to the ambulance driver who had "superguts," as one cop put it, and was about to

53

go back upstairs to the seventh floor of Charity when a buzz of shouts, screams, and panic spread through the emergency waiting room.

"He's shooting at the hospital ramp!" an excited nurse screamed as she ran back inside. Doctors, security police, nurse's aides, bystanders, and the curious had from time to time during the afternoon gone out to the emergency ramp to catch a bit of the action—to see if they could see the man (or men) who were terrorizing and paralyzing an entire city. Apparently the killer spotted them there and fired a number of shots at the general area. The emergency ramp was clear of people for the rest of the afternoon and evening.

I found Judy Persigo, the wife of Paul, sitting in a daze with her father and brother-in-law, Mike Kahrs. Gently, I took her to a small room and broke the terrible news that Paul was dead. Stunned, she looked at my hand. There was blood on my fingers.

"Is—is that Paul's blood?" she whispered.

"I—I don't know, Judy. For a while there I prayed over and anointed so many men that I'm not sure. But one thing I am certain of: it's hero's blood."

For a long time Judy sat there with her eyes closed. "You know," she said softly, "today's my birthday—" And then her head bowed and I heard deep, racking sobs. I called in her dad and Mike, good and gentle people whose lives—like Judy's—had been shattered by a cruel and senseless .44 magnum bullet.

Archbishop Philip Hannan and I visited Judy at home later that night. Her pink birthday cake was still on the table, but there were no candles for her or for her three little children to blow out. They were already out.

Silently, cautiously, the five policemen, led by Chief Louis Sirgo, had begun their climb to attempt to free their fellow officers in the stalled elevator on the eighteenth floor: Jules Killelea, whom Sirgo had asked to be his aide when Sirgo was appointed chief; Sgt. Freddie Williams, Lt. John LoPinto, Sgt. Bernard Flint, and Det. Walter Averett. All had volunteered to go with Sirgo, and they began their ascent in total darkness after Sirgo had cautioned, "No flashlights; turn off your radios!"

It was about 1:00 P.M., but on that south stairwell of the Howard Johnson Motel, it might as well have been midnight. The four men, on their mission of mercy, carried their shotguns at ready position. The silence, the darkness, was eerie.

At the tenth floor, Sirgo stopped and whispered, "Let's take a breath here."

After a brief pause, the silent climb continued. With Sirgo in the lead, they pushed on. The only light came from an open door far, far below them. At the fifteenth floor, Chief Sirgo, weapon in hand, turned at the landing with his left foot on the first step.

A horrendous roar suddenly exploded from above. Chief Louis Sirgo fell to the ground and mumbled, "My Jesus, I'm dying—my Jesus, I'm dying!"—the last words he would ever utter.

Killelea, immediately behind Sirgo, pumped three shotgun blasts one floor above him into the darkness. He quickly handed his gun to Williams and picked up his boss and friend and carried him down to the landing below.

One of them radioed to Command Desk. "Signal red! Signal red! The chief's been hit!" The three policemen picked up Sirgo's limp and bleeding body, and hurried down to the ground floor and a waiting unit.

Chief Louis Sirgo, that gentle and good man, was pronounced dead on arrival at Charity Hospital. A cruel .44 blast had torn into his back and punctured his lungs.

Later that sad afternoon, Patrolman Larry Arthur spotted the suspect and chased him up the stairs leading to the roof of the motel. He saw a door on the Perdido Street side and pried it open. There was a thunderous shot and Arthur felt a .44 magnum tearing into him. He was carrying Chief Sirgo's shotgun, which had been left in the stairwell after the chief had been shot. The gun fell from his hands in between the door and the doorjamb—wedging it open. Two of his buddies later got to Larry, and in a short time he was in Charity's emergency room, where his condition was listed as "serious, but stable."

And as the long, bloody afternoon wore on into evening, powerful spotlights bathed a foggy New Orleans night in glaring, unrelenting light, searching for the elusive gunman—or gunmen. The world tallied the ghastly, crimson-red scoreboard, which read: 7 KILLED—11 WOUNDED.

At 8:00 P.M., a military helicopter carrying police sharpshooters was called into action by the police. Piloted by Marine Lt. Col. "Chuck" Pitman, the helicopter began circling the cement cubicle on the roof where Mark Essex had taken refuge. On its second pass, the killer emerged and fired a volley of .44 magnum bullets, one of which hit the chopper just inches above the pilot's head. There was a brief landing nearby to check the damage, then the chopper took off again—and the drama of the Howard Johnson Motel tragedy was about to end in a final wild crescendo.

Mark "Jimmy" Essex, in a letter to television station WWL postmarked just four days before, had told about the New Year's Eve attack on police headquarters when he wrote:

Africa greets you December 31, 1972, Appt. [sic] 11 the New Orleans Police Department will be attacked. Reason—many.

But the death of two innocent brothers will be avenged, and many others.

P.S. Tell Pig Giarrusso the Felong Action Squad Ain't

[signed] Mata

Perhaps words like these were on his lips as he dashed once again from his shelter on the roof as the helicopter passed close above him at 8:50 P.M. He was screaming, shouting, and cursing. He raised the deadly .44 magnum rifle again for the last time. A hail of lead from the rifles of the officers in the chopper cut through his body as he screamed his final curse to the world.

It was 9:00 P.M.—about ten hours since Mark Essex had first entered the motel. Now he lay sprawled on the roof, cold and silent and stilled. His life was over.

But were there others?

The debate raged on. *Were* there more accomplices? The reports were unbelievably contradictory—reports like these:

"Reliable sources," positioned on the Federal Building, said that a second person could periodically be seen on the roof after Essex took refuge in the cubicle. But at 2:00 P.M. the following day (Monday), a group of police, volunteers all, stormed the roof from both the Perdido Street and Gravier Street sides and found no one except the lifeless body of ex-navy man Mark Essex and eighteen used cartridges from a .44 caliber magnum rifle.

When officers later searched the apartment of Mark Essex (his family called him "Jimmy"), located at 2619½ Perdido Street, they found his walls painted with antiwhite slogans calling for black supremacy and black revolution. Officers also found a map of the city with police headquarters and the Howard Johnson Motel circled in red.

Subsequent evidence showed that Essex had gained entrance to the motel by running up the stairwell after he parked his stolen car on the fourth floor of the garage area. No evidence of forced entry was found on the eighteenth floor, yet normally the door was kept locked. This led to the conclusion that it was either unintentionally left un-locked or that it was opened by someone from the inside.

In all, a minimum of eighty-three .44 caliber magnum shells were recovered, fifty-one of which had been fired.

There were many witnesses who had seen Essex on or before January 7, 1973—thirty-four to be exact. And in each instance, according to the testimony, Essex was alone. At no time did any witness observe Mark Essex in the company of another person.

Still the debate roars on: Were there others? Perhaps the world will never know.

For the next three days and nights, I shared the grief of the families of the dead policemen and civilians while keeping daily vigil at the bedsides of the wounded victims in hospitals, including Sgt. Ed Hosli, shot one week earlier at the warehouse.

On the day that Phil Coleman was buried, police and FBI examined the room where Mark "Jimmy" Essex had lived. Some of the slogans that were found on the wall may well give some clues to the extreme, bottled-up hatred which motivated the killing and wounding of so many people. Printed in red and black was a litany of hate—a litany that exploded into tragedy.

Along with Muslim newspaper clippings on the wall were these slogans:

1. Revolutionary Justice.
2. Political Power Comes from the Barrel of a Gun
3. My Destiny Lies in the Bloody Death of Racist Pigs
4. Kill White Devil and Kill White Pig
5. Hate White People—Beast of the Earth

Essex's mother, in an interview with the national press, claimed, among other things, that the tragic deaths were "a clear signal for white America to get off their tails and do something." She also added that her son Jimmy did not hate white men; he hated what the white man stood for. He hated the white system. He knew whites; dated a white girl. He was a good boy, she went on, but his trouble had started with the navy, which she claimed had brainwashed him.

I had just finished reading Mrs. Essex's reflections when I remembered that Paul Persigo, who was killed by Essex, had been a proud member of one of the police honor guards at the funeral of his friend, Alfred Harrell, the black police cadet who had been killed by Essex just one week earlier.

On the rainy morning that Persigo was laid to rest, I walked through the mud in the Garden of Memories Cemetery with a leaden heart. Paul's family and friends, an honor guard of police, men from his district, and his partner, Joe Verna, also plodded from the cars to the spot where Paul would find rest and peace. The requiem mass at St. Edward's Church, Paul's parish, had been concelebrated by Archbishop Hannan, myself, and his pastor.

Paul's widow, Judy, head held high, kept her eyes on the casket carried just ahead of her by six of Paul's fellow officers. I watched her two older children, who were holding her hand; their faces were pinched and pale, their wide eyes uncomprehending. It was obvious that they were having difficulty trying to accept the fact that this was *their* daddy they were putting in the ground.

And then I looked down at little Holly, whose hand was in mine. The child, with her braces secured on tiny legs, was gamely, grimly, hobbling to her father's grave. And trying not to cry.

59

Vested in cassock and white surplice, I bent down low to whisper to her, as she trudged by my side. "Holly, let me carry you the rest of the way."

Eyes glazed with an unknown hurt and pain looked up at me. "No, thank you. I always liked to walk with my daddy. He had to wait for me sometimes."

She swallowed and looked down at the cemetery's mud and pebbles. Then she looked up with a tiny smile, and her eyes filled with tears as she said, "And you know what? Daddy was going to teach me how to *run!* —Honest!"

As I squeezed her little hand, tears rolled unashamedly down my face onto the open ritual and across the words, "I am the Resurrection and the Life. He who believes in Me will live forever. . . ."

CHAPTER 6

The Tale of a Cup of Coffee

4:52 P.M.

THE PRIEST, MINISTER, OR RABBI in the average American parish handles a number of exciting and fascinating cases in his ministry. In the average rectory or parish house, there are very few dull or boring moments. Or at least there shouldn't be, if everyone is doing his job.

But the life of a police or fire chaplain in a large, metropolitan port city is something else. True, he performs the regular and routine duties of any pastor: he celebrates the Supper of the Lord for the people of God every day (sometimes twice or three times daily); he hears confessions; makes hospital calls; buries the dead; sets up poverty programs for the poor; helps run the bingo games; directs the parish school; worries about and tries to manage a budget; has charge of a number of societies in the parish; prepares his Sunday homily and then tries to deliver it as best he can. He plays golf or goes fishing once in a while and likes to get away for a retreat and a vacation now and then. He enjoys a Scotch or two and deals a pretty fair hand of poker.

But there is more, lots more, in the life of a police chaplain—in any city, large or small.

I was driving back from Charity Hospital's emergency room at 4:52 on a Tuesday afternoon. I had just finished watching a group of skillful young surgeons and some expert nurses trying to save the life of a man who had had his stomach opened by a razor-sharp knife in a barroom brawl.

"Another cutting, this time black on black!" a young doctor muttered.

I squeezed into the all-too-small emergency room and looked at the naked man on the table under the bright lights with parts of him oozing out. Slipping behind a portly nurse, I administered the last rites to the dying victim: absolution, the holy oils (the Sacrament of the Sick), and gave the Last Blessing, asking the Saviour to comfort him, to strengthen him, to be close to him, to heal him in this hour of suffering. Then, bending low and close to his bloody ear I repeated, "Jesus, Mary, Joseph—my Jesus, I love you. My Jesus, I am sorry I have offended you. My Jesus, I love you. Forgive me—forgive me."

All the while, the team of surgeons were doing their job, efficiently, skillfully, with a minimum of talk. Blood was being given; probing hands and fingers went into the man's belly; other doctors felt his head and body for any additional wounds; oxygen was administered. I whispered a final, silent prayer to St. Jude for the man's recovery—or for his happy death—and slipped around the chubby nurse who whispered to me, with a poker face, "Better lose some of that weight, Reverend!"

After checking the victim's driver's license and ID, I dropped a nickel in the lobby phone and called the man's mother and asked her to come to the hospital. There had been an accident, I told her, and her son was involved.

"Yes, he's alive; I'll give you more details when you get here."

The mother and her eleven-year-old daughter Venezia arrived in a cab a half hour later. I guided them past and in and out of the long lines of people waiting patiently to see a doctor and took them into one of the medical offices. After she sat down, I told the woman as gently as possible that her son had been stabbed in Lucy's Corner Bar. He was still living, I assured her, but was in pretty bad shape. I told her that some of the best doctors in the world were in there now, fighting with all their talent and skill to keep him alive. And I reminded her that prayer was now the best medicine around.

The woman listened with wide, fear-filled eyes that would glide past me from time to time as if she were thinking about something that had happened a long, long time ago. Finally she whispered, "I tol' that boy to stay outta that barroom—I tol' him, I tol' him, I tol' him—"

As I took her hand and squeezed it sympathetically, she sank back into the chair and continued to stare past me at nothing, tearing a Kleenex into shreds. Her little girl watched impassively, shyly rolling her huge eyes up to mine occasionally and then quickly looking away.

Later, out in the visitors' waiting room, I offered to drive them home, but they decided to wait it out. With a promise to check in later on, I left.

It had been a long day and I was tired. It would be nice to get home, fix a cold martini, and watch the six-o'clock news on TV. Heading for Rampart Street, I heard the dispatcher on Channel 1 telling anybody who was listening that Car 30 was wanted up on St. Charles and Sixth; it was a 27-29-S—a woman threatening suicide.

I flipped on the blue police lights and, holding the screaming siren button in my left hand, took off for St. Charles. Ten minutes later my white Ford pulled to a halt across the street from where a sizable group of people were staring up at an open window on the sixth floor of an eight-story apartment building. On the sidewalk below, firemen were holding a jump net under the open window. Climbing from the car, I clenched my teeth as I heard the all-too-familiar shouts and taunts and laughter from the crowd: "Go ahead 'n jump, you chicken-livered broad!"

"Fifty to one you don't do it!"

"Come on down—the sidewalk's fine!"

As many times as I have heard these shouts from the crowds at a suicide scene, my blood always boils and

63

rages. The pages of the Bible come agonizingly alive as I think of the hate-inspired taunts of the mob demanding the release of Barabbas—and the death of the innocent Saviour.

A woman suddenly appeared in the window on the sixth floor. Her graying hair was disarranged; she looked dazed. As I was tucking the black kit that contained the holy oils under my arm, I saw a fat, sloppy man sitting on the curb nearby with a couple of his drinking buddies. Dirty undershirt. Unshaven. Unemployment check sticking out of his back pocket. He opened another beer from the six-pack, put it by his side, laughed loudly, and screamed up to the woman at the window, "Go ahead—I dare ya! Ya haven't got the guts! You're a m—— f——!"

Suddenly he looked down sharply as he felt cold beer seeping onto the seat of his dirty trousers. He looked up in anger. "What the hell do—?" When he saw the black-suited figure standing over him, his mouth hung open.

I smiled at him. "Sorry about that. I was so busy *listening* to you that I didn't see your beer sitting there. Y'know, pal, if you really wanted to do something *good*—which I seriously doubt—you might offer that poor woman one of those beers. Or better still, offer her a little prayer."

Fatso's mouth opened, but no words came out as my eyes met his—and held them for a moment until he looked away.

I walked over to the apartment entrance and was briefed by Lt. Van Flynn of the Second District.

"We can't get at her, Father. She's got herself locked in. Her husband is here someplace; they've been separated for a couple of years. She spent the last six months across the lake at Mandeville Sanitarium. Apparently she flipped early this morning. Want to go up?"

"Yeah, Van. An audience like that would drive anyone out a window."

We looked over at the crowd, laughing and treating the whole thing like a picnic at Pontchartrain Beach, like a Barnum & Bailey Circus with the big, final act about to come up. Van Flynn looked at the now-quiet fat man and smiled. "Poor fella, he lost his beer. And you didn't get any on your shoe, either—let's go, Padre."

We took the elevator to the sixth and Van Flynn pointed out the door. "Her name is Agnes—Agnes Merrett. About fifty years old; she's a pretty sick woman. I'll be downstairs if you need me. She don't want to see *me*." And the lieutenant left.

I knocked on Agnes' door. No answer. I knocked again—louder.

"Agnes?—Agnes?"

After a moment the response came. "Whatdaya want?"

"Can you hear me, Agnes? I'm a priest. My name is Father Pete. I want to have a little talk with you—I'm your friend. Can we talk for a minute?"

I continued this approach, shouting through the locked door as persuasively and earnestly as I could. Finally, taking a plastic holy picture of St. Jude with the prayer "Don't Quit" on the reverse side, I slipped it under the door. "Agnes, that's a picture of Saint Jude. He's your friend, too. Let me in and we'll talk. We can help you. You can trust me."

The picture card came flying back under the door. "I don't need no goddamn preacher to tell me I'm nuts, 'cause I'm *not*. Do you hear me, *I'm not!*"

" 'Course you're not, Agnes." And St. Jude quietly went under the door again into the woman's room.

She moved away from the door, possibly to the window, I guessed.

"—and if they try to break in the door, I'm out the window. Tell them that, *priest!*"

"There is no one here but me, Agnes." In a firm, conspiratorial voice I added, "Can I tell you something—just between you and me?"

Woman's curiosity moved her back to the door. "What?"

"My mother's name was Agnes. It's—it's a very pretty name."

Silence.

"Do you like your name? Do you know what it means?"

Silence.

"It means 'little lamb.' Did you know that?"

"No." The voice sounded very small.

"Well, it does. Say, is that coffee I smell?"

"Yes, there's a pot on the stove."

"Agnes—do you like to bet?"

Silence.

"I'll bet you a quarter that I can make a better cup of coffee than you. Want to try?"

Silence.

Above my racing pulse I could almost hear her thinking, deciding.

Dear Saint Jude, I prayed, say something for me, will you? And make it the right thing, please.

I heard the words come out, "Agnes, I do believe you'd win the bet. It smells like very good coffee in there."

More silence.

As I stood motionless, with pounding heart and an ear up tight against the door, the story that I had heard of a police chaplain in San Francisco somehow flashed through my mind. He was trying to talk a deranged woman out of suicide by telling her that if she did jump she would be arrested.

"Arrested?" The woman almost laughed. "If I jump, it's twenty stories down. I'd be dead. What would they arrest me for?"

"*Littering!*" responded the chaplain. And as she laughed and relaxed, the woman soon agreed to come down and talk with him.

"Sir?" Agnes asked, in her little-girl voice. "Are you alone?"

Moments later, five locks were slipped open, turned, released, unchained, and the final one unbolted. And then she opened the door for a curious look at the man who thought he could make a better cup of coffee than she.

I entered the cluttered and disarrayed apartment, went to the window and waved the firemen and their net away. I looked around the room and picked up a large pair of scissors lying on the sofa, then casually sat down between her and the window. "Now, Agnes, about that coffee—"

As in the case of each suicide attempt, we began to talk first about everything and anything except why she wanted to go out the window; little inconsequential things. Slowly we came around to what a precious and lovely thing life is and how we have to take care of it. She was crying as she poured the thick, black goop into my cup. "They—my husband and them—never did like me. They never wanted me to get out of the hospital. Nobody ever loved me."

"Wow, but you're wrong. God loves you—very much. He loves you so much that he sent Saint Jude and me to help you this afternoon. He wants us to help you pick up the pieces, Agnes, and begin putting them all together again, nice and slow, just like I'm putting sugar in this cup of coffee—nice and slow." I let a teaspoon of sugar spill slowly into the murky depths of the soiled cup. "And you know what? Saint Jude is asking you to read the prayer that's on the back of the card I slipped under your door. Would you, please?"

"Don't quit . . ." she began in a tiny voice, like a seventh-grade schoolgirl reciting in front of the boys. One hand held her frayed robe across her pitifully thin chest.

When things go wrong as they sometimes will,
When the road you're trudging seems all uphill,

> When the funds are low and the debts are high,
> And you want to smile, but you have to sigh,
> When care is pressing you down a bit,
> Rest, if you must, but *don't you quit.*

And then she burst out in a piercing cry, "Oh, please help me!" And she ran to me.

I cradled the poor, unloved and unwanted woman in my arms for some time. When her sobbing ceased, she looked up at me and managed a half-smile. "You know, I like what you said before—that God never makes *junk*. I always—they always—thought I was *junk*—but I'm not!"

"O.K. Agnes. We're going to talk more later. Right now, I want you to try *my* coffee. Come with me to the rectory at Saint Jude's, and we'll see who wins the bet. But I can tell you right now, you've got a big lead. Put your coat on, take your purse, and we'll lock up again. I have a wonderful friend I'd like you to meet. He's also a very good doctor, but he makes lousy coffee."

I thought about what the much-publicized "hostage cop," Lt. Frank Bolz of the NYPD, had to say about what a cop named Harvey Schlossberg (who had a Ph.D. in psychology) thought. In an article about Bolz in *True* magazine (February 1976) Bolz said he agreed with Schlossberg, who stated, concerning a hostage or critical situation:

We also have a policy where we do not bring relatives or *clergy* to the scene to appeal to the perpetrator. . . . Clergy have a tendency to *depress* the person, to make him feel guilty or negative about himself. . . . We had a case in the Bronx that wound up being a barricaded psycho with a rifle to his chin. . . . Someone decided, "Let's bring in the clergy," and all the clergy talked about was how it's a sin to commit suicide and you burn in hell and everything else; and he got angry at this priest and started throwing things at him. . . . [Italics mine.]

I couldn't *disagree* more with Dr. Schlossberg and/or Lieutenant Bolz. Or maybe they got the wrong "clergy."

Agnes, with her disturbed mind now zeroing in on other things, began to hum, "Let's have a second cup of coffee—" And I sang, "and let's have another piece of pie."

As she put her frail hand to her hair, she looked at me and said happily, "Let's go, sir. I think I am going to win twenty-five cents."

As we left for the rectory and help for her disturbed mind, she giggled like a little girl who had a very special secret.

CHAPTER 7

The Coca-Cola Collectible

12:55 P.M.

THE OBLATES WERE SITTING in the community room at Guadalupe. It was our monthly day of retreat.

Once a month, in all the Oblate districts of the world, the priests and brothers get together. We pray together; we reassess the job we are trying to do; we share some theological and biblical reflections.

Following a concelebrated mass and some time in prayer, we enjoy a Scotch or two, a meal, and some fine, deep fellowship. The fraternity and camaraderie that exist among Oblates all over the world is a very warm and precious thing. It was one of the main reasons that many of us chose this congregation.

After the serious work is over, they know how to enjoy a laugh and swap some stories. Fr. John Courchesne was wrapping up an anecdote when the buzzer rang in the community room.

"Someone at the front door to see you, Father," the receptionist phoned.

"Tell them I'll be right down."

"The man says it's urgent."

"I'll be down in two minutes."

"It's Mike Mellon."

"Be right there."

As I left, I heard Courchesne on his punch line. "And God the Holy Spirit then said to God the Father. 'Oh, yes—I remember John. He was the one who invited me to a council that he had called—and I forgot to go!"

Mike Mellon was sitting outside the front door on the steps. His face was bloody. He held a dirty handkerchief to his face. His eyes were blazing. He was carrying something in a crumpled paper bag.

"God, Mike, come in!—What happened?"

"Jeez, Padre. Willya tell them guys to get off my ass!"

"What guys?"

"Those bastard cops! I'm trying to do right; trying to make it straight. Every time a certain couple of them sees me, they stop me, frisk me, rough me up, and threaten to send me back to the slammer. And I don't do nothin'—honest to God!"

I led Mike into the office and sat him down. I gave him a towel to clean his face, got him some ice and a cup of black coffee.

"Tell me about it."

It was four years earlier that Mike Mellon had been persuaded to give himself up in the Dream Girl barroom shoot-out. On that night, I had promised to stick with him. I visited him in the old Parish Prison, a jail which should have been awarded top honors for one of the nation's worst and most overcrowded. I stuck with him during those bleak days seeing, among other things, that the wound on his face was treated promptly and properly and, with the help of cooperative Sheriff Charles Foti, had gotten Linda in to see Mike.

The indigent defender—the lawyer who had been assigned to the case—and I talked at length about Mike. There is a pool of attorneys, funded by a federal grant, that defends the poor who are unable to afford a lawyer. When Mike's trial finally came up, I personally talked to the DA assigned to his case and then to the judge and gave them background on the young man—and stressed again how I believed in him.

I am no bleeding heart who wants to open up every jail

cell door in America, but I sincerely thought we could work with this kid and return him to society as a useful and productive citizen. We discussed the background of Stoppio, the owner of the bar who had tried to seduce Mike's wife. I pointed out how Mike was then out of work and, with the added fear of losing his wife, had gone on a beer-drinking spree. His mixed-up mind decided that the only way out was to shoot Stoppio. But, I pointed out, he *didn't*.

The charge was reduced from attempted murder to shooting firearms illegally, disturbing the peace, and interfering with the police. He was sentenced to five years in Angola State Prison.

Mike kept his nose clean and did a good job at Angola— mainly because interested people kept close tabs on him. Not only did I write and communicate with him, but I visited him and asked the prison chaplain to stay in close contact with him. When the chance came for him to be sent to DeQuincy, a more modern institution for first offenders, I again went to bat for him, and he was soon transferred there. Mike was assigned to work on the prison farm, and his record was good.

After another year and a half, he was eligible for parole, and again I appeared before the State Board of Pardons and pleaded for a parole.

All because I *believed* in the kid.

On May 8, I drove to DeQuincy and appeared for the last time before the State Parole Board. Formally petitioning that Mike Mellon be granted a parole and release, I promised to be his "guardian." I had already obtained a fairly good job for Mike as a painter at the Vieux Carre Motor Lodge here in New Orleans, where genial Gardiner Boulmey had promised to put him to work. I had also helped Linda get a nice, clean, and inexpensive apartment uptown and a job at Woolworth's.

When his parole was granted, my heart sang with happiness as I broke the good news to an excited Linda.

Religiously, Mike dropped by the rectory and visited once a week. I kept in touch with Mr. Boulmey and was assured that the young man was doing very well at his job. Then, one day, six months later, with Linda on his arm, he announced proudly that a son was to be born—a little Mike Mellon.

The world was looking bright once again. The infamous night in the Dream Girl bar was over; the torturous nights and days in Parish Prison, in Angola, in DeQuincy, were now just haunting memories of a bad yesterday.

Now, as I sat Mike down on the sofa in my office, I remembered a fearful phone call that I had gotten from a K & B drugstore two months ago. It was Mike. He claimed that two policemen had stopped him again on the street, and fearing what was coming, he turned and ran. They caught him in an alley and beat him. They called him a cop-killer, a jail fink, a bastard, and a few other choice things. They threatened, Mike claimed, that they would see him back in Angola. And when he got there, they had "friends" inside the prison system who would kill him.

And today it had happened again.

"But why?" Mike looked up with fearful eyes, holding the ice to his jaw. "How the hell long is this going to go on? I'm trying to go straight."

"Mike," I tried to explain, "when you once shoot at policemen, some have a tendency never to forget that you at one time tried to kill them. You know and I know that you were not out to kill any police that night on Canal Street— but *they* don't know it. They've got wives and kids, too, you know? Just like you and Linda. I've got to admit that some cops, depending on their background and their education and their personality, are over-aggressive, some even brutal. But believe me, Mike, most of them are pretty balanced guys with a tough job to do. Did you ever stop to think what a cop has to take today?

"There's a policeman around named Keith Wilkins. He's a good, decent family man, and he says that a policeman often feels like a Jekyll-Hyde character: when he's on duty and when he's off duty. Policemen have to form their own society. 'In a way, it's us against the world,' he said. 'If we don't take care of ourselves, no one else will.'

"You see, Mike, it's almost impossible for outsiders to understand or to break into the world of the police, and it's almost as hard for a rookie policeman. Sometimes—many times—even their wives can't understand the change in their thinking, their philosophy.

"When you join the force, you go through a severe identity crisis. Your uniform puts you into the police community which can't accept you yet, and you've been rejected by society because you're one of *them*. You're somewhere between death and rebirth: you're in limbo, where no one accepts you.

"It's a darn tough life for a man, Mike. They are shorthanded; their pay is low; they live a dangerous life. They deal twenty-four hours a day with the dregs of a sick society.

"We have good cops and we have bad cops. We have some of the finest men I have ever known—anyplace—and we have some—very few—of the biggest thieves. We have honest police; we have some crooked police. We have homosexual cops; we have some officers on drugs. We have brutal ones, and we have the most gentle men I've ever met.

"But the main point, Mike, is that, by far, the large majority of them are *good;* trying to do one helluva job for a community that really doesn't care, for a pitiful salary that's less than a bus driver's!

"And Mike—" I looked him directly in the eye, "I *believe*

in the vast majority of them so much that I'd put my life on the line for them—just like I believe in you. Just like I put my life on the line for you.

"That night in the Dream Girl, if one of your shots had hit one of them, there would have been a widow and kids without a father. Don't you see? They—some of them, anyway—think that you are their enemy; that you still might be out to kill. They don't know you like I know you."

"But I *didn't* try to kill anybody. I was so screwed up—so mixed up—so goddamned bombed out of my mind that I only wanted to get a hold of Stoppio. Can't they believe that?" He sat holding the ice to his head for a long time. "So what am I gonna do—dig a hole and die?"

"No, Mike. But for now, do me a favor and stay out of the First District. That's where all the humbug—the trouble—took place. Don't walk around laughing, as it were, in their faces. Don't wave a red flag at them.

"You once told me that Linda's sister in Chicago wants you to go up there when the baby is born. Are you still thinking about that?"

Mellon smiled for the first time. "Yeah, we've been thinking about it. We saved a little money and her sister's husband—believe it or not—is a Chicago cop. A helluva nice guy. And he found me a good job there. After the baby is born and baptized," and he looked up with shining eyes, "by *you,* I think we'll head out."

As he rose to leave, Mike turned and said, "Oh—I almost forgot. I brought you a present. From me and Linda. You see, after work I go into the French Quarter, where they are doing a lot of excavating. I'm a bottle hunter. You find lots of good things down deep in the dirt. I sell the bottles to antique dealers. So I brought you this."

And he took a grimy, dust-filled bottle from the crumpled brown bag.

"It's for you, Father," Mike beamed proudly. "It's a 1915

Coca-Cola bottle. Very rare. It—it says a lot of things, but most of all it says 'thanks'—for everything—from the three of us." And Mike Mellon shook my hand, turned, and left.

And to this day that old 1915 Coke bottle is more precious to me than the rarest Grecian vase.

CHAPTER 8

The Lady Who Lived in the Past

4:05 P.M.

MRS. MELANIE RUBY COOPER was a sweet little old lady—a sweet little old lady who had just celebrated her eighty-sixth birthday. She lived alone in a two-story frame house that belonged to Octave, her son. Other tenants, a "bunch of nosy people," lived downstairs.

Mrs. Cooper had always led a very active life, but for the past ten years, she didn't get to do as much as she used to. Her daughter-in-law did the shopping for her once a week (on Tuesdays), and she was only able to go to church when they picked her up and took her.

"Lan's sake, they treat me like a baby" was her perpetual complaint.

She was fiercely independent; she would not live with any of her family, despite all Octave's objections. Every day she would sit on her upstairs front porch and watch the traffic go by on Magazine Street. Later she would go inside, turn on the TV, and watch her favorite program, "As the World Turns." She was always a bit confused trying to keep up with who was divorcing whom, but she liked the nice young doctors who were always making medical and marital mistakes. Sometimes they made very bad mistakes, but they were still very nice.

Then, about four in the afternoon, Melanie Ruby Cooper would take her little trip back into the past. She would get one of her boxes of old letters, her husband's wedding band, and some nostalgic trivia from long, long ago. She would examine the box with its "official" papers, her burial insurance policy with Laughlin Funeral Home, and some old faded photos of when she and her husband took trips over to Biloxi back in 1915.

"Lan's sake, those were the days. All the young men then looked like the nice young doctors do now on TV," she would muse.

And then daily about 4:30, sweet Mrs. Cooper would go to a secret place and get her hidden bottle of bourbon and toss down two or three slugs: straight. The nice grocery boy would buy it for her; she would tip him a dime; and no one ever knew. The frail old lady would then live in the dreamy past for the next hour or two, and when the cool breezes from the river came in, she would awaken from her reverie, wash out the glass, and return the bottle and the box to the special hiding-place where no one, not even her daughter-in-law, would find it.

That was *her* secret, and no one could share it; those glorious, beautiful years when she enjoyed youth and fun and life and love and adventure. Lately though, she noticed that after the bourbon she had been falling asleep a bit faster and for a longer time. Two weeks ago she found a pot of beans afire on the stove when she awoke.

"Lan's sake, I must watch that," she would say.

As I wheeled Car 30, with siren screaming and blue lights flashing, to the 311 fire on Magazine Street, I found myself wondering what kind of fire it would be. And as on every call, I prayed for our firefighters who would be fighting that blaze, and I prayed also for any victims of that fire. The fire dispatcher only knew when he called that it was a wooden two-story residence with supposedly one person trapped inside the building.

As I eased Car 30 alongside a pumper, about a half-block from the scene on Magazine Street, I saw that the fire had spread from the two-story frame residence on

Magazine to the houses behind, and most of the firemen had been diverted to moving ladders and attacking the new threat to the rear. There was an entire block of wooden houses to the back; if the fire got out of control there, that complete block might be wiped out.

Billows of smoke still poured from the upstairs section of the apartment on Magazine Street, although apparently the fire was out. As I approached the house, wearing the chaplain's orange fire coat with the black cross on the back, an excited neighbor grabbed my arm.

"Sir, sir—the old lady just went back up there! She's back *up* there!"

I assured the person that there were firemen there and that she would be escorted out again in a moment.

"But the firemen aren't there. They all went to the back to get at the new fire. Please get them. Poor Mrs. Cooper is senile; she doesn't really know what's going on. We live downstairs. They had taken her out once, but she wandered back up there!"

I decided that too much time would be spent in running to the rear and getting help. Buttoning my fire coat and pulling up the boots, I grasped the holy oil kit and made my way into the smoke-filled house. The smoke was not too bad downstairs, and once I found the stairway, I groped my way up to the second floor.

"Mrs. Cooper! Mrs. Cooper!" I yelled at the top of the stairs.

I opened the first door on the right and found myself in what looked like the living room. I turned left and made my way to the kitchen which was totally charred; apparently food burning on the stove had started the fire. No one was there and I went toward the front to the bedroom. That's where I stumbled on the old lady, down on her knees, trying to open the bottom drawer of an ancient dresser.

"Will you help me, young man?" she asked, "I've misplaced a box. It's my jewelry, my husband's wedding ring, and some papers. I must find it. And there was also a little money and some snapshots."

I looked around and saw nothing. Only a half-empty bourbon bottle on the table.

"Lady, we've got to get out of here. This smoke is very bad for you. Besides, that ceiling looks like it's about to fall in any minute."

"Lan's sake, I wonder what I did with my little box?" The old woman, completely oblivious to the smoke and the noise and the crackling of the fire next door, rambled on. "I know it's here someplace. I was looking through it a little while ago, but can't find it now. Can't find anything anymore. And the ring—my late husband's ring—"

"Mrs. Cooper, if we both don't get out of here now, you won't have to worry about finding anything anymore."

"You go right ahead, young man. I'm going to find it if it's the last thing I do."

"Listen to me. My name is Father Rogers. I'm a priest and the chaplain of the fire department. Now, I'm not asking you anymore; I'm telling you—we're leaving! *Now*, Mrs. Cooper!"

The disturbed woman began to cry. "Mr. Cooper gave it to me a long time ago—after a trip to Biloxi. I'd like you to see it."

"After the danger is over, we'll come back up here together and I'll help you find it. Can we go now, please?"

Mrs. Cooper wasn't listening. The smoke from the burning roof of the house to the rear was now pouring in through Mrs. Cooper's back windows. I took out a handkerchief and breathed through it. The acrid smoke seared my lungs and stung my eyes. I wet a kitchen towel and handed it to her, but the old lady didn't seem the least bit bothered.

When she started back toward the kitchen, groping and

stumbling, I made the decision. Suddenly swooping her into my arms, I headed for the door. Surprised and furious, the woman began to beat my chest and helmet with weak, childlike blows.

Water was dripping from the sagging ceiling, and it looked like it might go at any moment. The tiny lady, whose thoughts were back sixty years ago, must not have weighed eighty pounds. As my unwilling passenger and I groped our way out the door to the hallway and the top of the stairs, suddenly there was a loud, crashing, swishing sound, and the ceiling of the bedroom came down with a roar. The stairs rocked and swayed for a dangerous moment but held in place.

Slowly I began to make my way down to the bottom; soothing, talking, and crooning to the old lady, who was crying, repeating over and over that she wanted to go back up.

Moments later, we were outside. The fresh air was beautiful.

Still half-blind from the smoke, I made my way across the street and out of danger with her in my arms. Some people who were standing on their porch ran to help. Setting her down on one of the rocking chairs, I gasped, "Would you watch her, please? Perhaps you could call her family." Wiping my burning eyes I looked at the old warrior. "Well, we made it, Mrs. Cooper. Would you like a glass of ice water?"

Melanie Ruby Cooper looked me straight in the eye. "Ice water? Lan's sake, young man, thank you, but no. But I wouldn't mind a bit of bourbon!"

I smiled. Melanie Ruby Cooper must have been some gal years ago. Matter of fact, she still was!

And I moved back toward the fire to join my troops.

CHAPTER 9

Flames Etch Deep Scars

5:35 P.M.

WHEN THE ENTIRE SCENE on Magazine Street was under control and the danger over, I returned to see how Melanie Ruby Cooper was making out.

Octave, her son, had arrived, and they were preparing to take her to his home for the night. Giving him my phone number, I put all the chaplain's gear in the car—helmet, fire coat, boots, and sick call set—and slowly headed back home.

Tired. Dead tired.

As I drove, my mind flashed back to some of the more serious fires that I had been called out on over the past years as chaplain of the New Orleans Fire Department.

And they were many.

Fires on ships docked in the busy port of New Orleans; fires in hotels; fires in wooden shacks in which the poor lived—and died; fires in automobiles; fires in churches and rectories, like the St. Louis Cathedral fire in the middle of the night, in which a horrible accident could easily have claimed the lives of four Oblate priests; fires on the top of buildings; fires at the racetrack.

I swung Car 30 over on Poydras Street and chuckled out loud as I recalled the fire at the racetrack.

It was 3:00 that morning, and I arrived at the track to find two large barns, which housed about forty racehorses, being devastated by a fiery blaze. It was fed by the old wooden structure, the hay inside—and a stiff breeze.

Father Rogers administers the last rites to a young woman whose nude and battered body was found behind a South Rampart Street saloon.

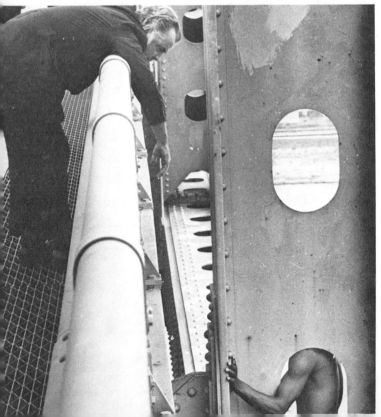

After listening to Father Rogers, the man on the
bridge decided not to jump into the Mississippi. The
man below, still deciding whether or not to jump
from the top of the Delta Towers, had to be tackled
by Rogers and wrestled to the roof.

This ninety-two-year-old woman insisted on going back into the burning building to retrieve her wedding ring. Father Rogers rescued her moments before the ceiling collapsed.

Moments after Patrolman Paul Persigo (standing with rifle) spoke to Father Rogers (kneeling at left), he was dead, shot in the face by the lone gunman roaming the floors of the Howard Johnson Motel.

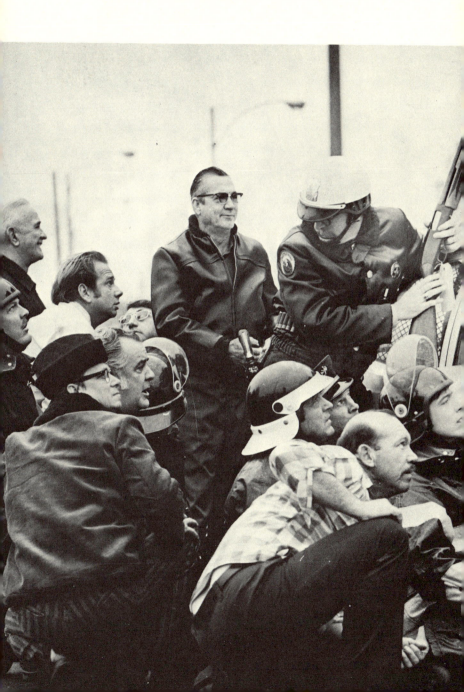

If the firefighter at the right had not shouted a warning, Father Rogers would have been crushed by the debris falling from a burning warehouse.

GLYNN BROWN

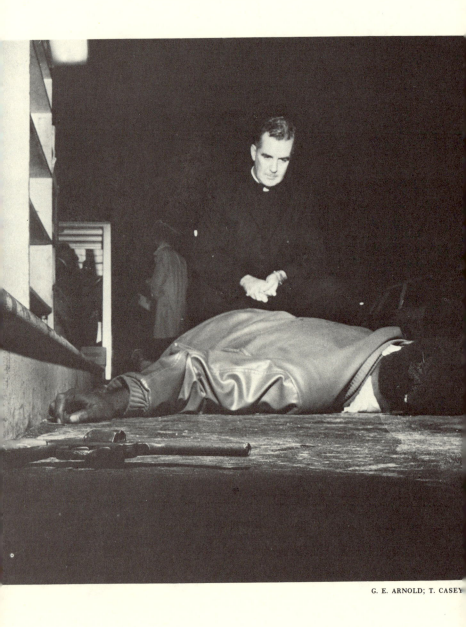

The rusty gun above was never fired—the holdup man
was killed. (*Opposite*): The well-oiled rifle went off by
accident; the old man tripped and fell. Father Rogers
gave the last rites to both men.

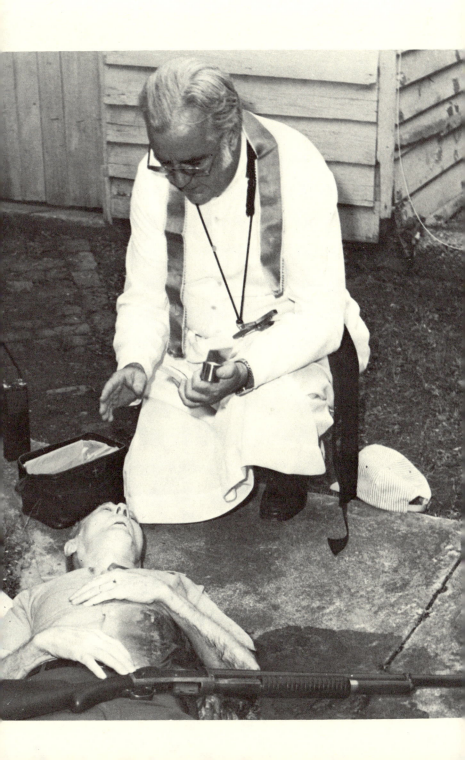

Last rites are administered to a firefighter killed when a building
on Dryades Street collapsed and to a seventy-eight-year-old man
knocked out of his shoes by a hit-and-run driver on
North Rampart Street

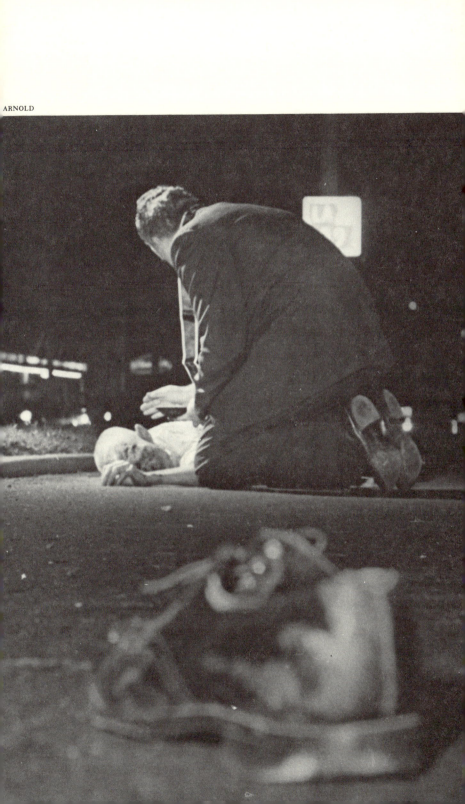

Most Police and Fire Department funerals are held at
Our Lady of Guadalupe. In progress here is a triple
funeral held for the three firefighters who had been
killed by a collapsing wall.

"Father," the district chief briefed me, "they tell me that a workout boy was asleep in there—in an empty stall. But we can't find him. We got most of the horses out; we only lost about five of them. Two that were badly burned had to be shot. I've got my men—"

At that moment, a young boy came running up and screamed at the chief, "He was my friend. He was good to me."

"Who was?" I asked.

"Timmy, the workout boy. He was going to teach me to become a jockey one day—and there he is." And the youngster pointed to a mound, about fifty yards away, covered with a tarpaulin.

A couple of firefighters, sweat and grime pouring from their faces, their hands blackened from their work, looked at the covered figure. They told their boss, "Dunno, Chief. He was lyin' there, all covered, when we got here. But a couple of the people who work here thought it was him . . ."

I quickly ran to where the corpse was lying, put the purple stole around my neck, removed my fire helmet, and knelt beside the charred heap, pulling back the tarpaulin slightly. A couple of firemen and the sobbing boy joined me in prayer and quietly watched as I placed the blessed oil on the protruding charred flesh and bone.

As I gave the Last Blessing and was halfway through the prayer, "Eternal rest grant unto him, O Lord," the kid suddenly jumped up as a figure approached from the shadows.

"Timmy—Timmy", he screamed. "Is—is it you?"

Yes, it was Timmy, the workout boy. He had left the stables that night to drink a few beers with some racetrack friends at the nearby Winner's Circle Lounge. Then he heard about the fire and came as fast as he could.

The victim?

I smiled as I remembered writing in my death register later that morning:

On the morning of March 2, at 4:05 A.M. I anointed the body of and administered the last rites to Lazy Tiger—a seven-year-old racehorse!

P.S. I hope he went to horse heaven, because I understand that more than a few of his backers had directed him to other regions following many of his recent races!

Driving the white Cobra and getting closer to the rectory on Rampart Street, I thought about the various types of alarms handled by our New Orleans Fire Department— one of the nation's finest firefighting organizations.

A first alarm, when a box is struck, is called a 111; a more serious fire graduates to a 211—a general alarm. When the conflagration is of a larger and more serious nature, a 311 is rung, and more equipment and more men are rushed to the scene. The fire chaplain is automatically called on every 311 or better. A 411 fire is a repeated general alarm; other companies move in, while the back-up people stand by. A 511 is the most serious fire of all. It is an all-out effort by the nation's finest firefighters to analyze, attack, and conquer one of man's deadliest enemies: an out-of-control fire.

The Rault Center fire on November 30, 1972 was a 511. And then some.

It happened at the top—the sixteenth story of the plush Rault Center office-apartment building where there was a popular restaurant called the Lamplighter Club. Right below, on the fifteenth floor, there was a beauty salon, also called the Lamplighter, and other offices. When the Rault Center fire broke out at 1:30 P.M. near the beauty shop, it spread rapidly.

Most of the diners in the restaurant and bar, one story above, headed for the stairs; some waited for the already overcrowded elevators to return and take them down. Someone in the crowd reportedly spread the rumor that one of the elevators had stalled on the tenth floor. At that point, about eight of the people decided to go up to the roof and sweat it out there.

The fire soon became a roaring and towering inferno, fed by beauty shop supplies, cans of hair spray, alcohol, and other combustibles on those floors. It raged more and more out of control, and its heat became more intense.

Large, thick window panes in the restaurant and club began to blow out, and huge pieces of glass, like hellish projectiles, hurtled down to the street below. One huge piece of this jagged glass missed one of the fire captains by a mere ten feet, severing dual fire hoses lying in the street like a razor cutting two strands of spaghetti.

Police struggled to push bystanders and the curious as far away from danger as possible.

As radio and TV bulletins spread the news of the holocaust, anguished friends and spouses began arriving, asking the chief, the police, the ambulance drivers, the Salvation Army, the chaplain, asking *anyone:* Had their wife or husband or friend been seen?

"She had an appointment for twelve noon in the beauty shop," cried one fearful husband. "Have they gotten out?"

The terrible answer soon came.

High above the street, in the Lamplighter Beauty Salon, a series of periodic explosions blocked the exits and trapped patrons and employees. There remained only one way out: the windows. Firemen raced to get ladders up to them from the roofs of adjoining buildings to the flaming fifteenth floor. They were just a few floors too short.

Deputy Chief Bill McCrossen, who is the present superintendent, was on top of the neighboring Traveller's Insurance Building and watched with a sickening feeling as the ladders fell short of the blazing windows. His men then began shooting fire lines—lines of string attached to stronger life lines—into the windows. But the victims were in such a state that they either didn't see them or didn't know what to do with them.

Two helicopters later flew near the roof, with incredible danger to both the choppers and their pilots, finally landing on the top of the skyscraper. There are people alive today who owe their lives to the heroism of pilots John Lockwood and Albert Carriger, who heard of the fire while flying on other duties. They both immediately headed to the Rault Center to aid in rescue efforts and landed in dense smoke on top of the burning building.

To this day, grizzled veteran firefighters with years of experience in attacking every form of fire still shudder as they recall the sound and the sight of women's bodies thudding with ghastly impact on the nearby roofs. Firemen still wake up in the night seeing them—women's bodies crashing on the roof not far from them.

People on the street below screamed; many fainted at the sight of these women who, in a last frantic, desperate fight for life, would crawl out on the ledge of the beauty shop and then slip, jump, or fall to the roofs of the adjacent building.

"There was no way that a net could have been used," recalls then-Fire Supt. Louis San Salvador. "A net could not have caught and held a human body hurtling to the ground at that speed, from that height."

Deputy Chief Fred Reiser pointed out that an average human body falling nine stories would be speeding through the air at sixty miles per hour, with an impact of four to six tons. In addition, the firemen holding the net would most probably also have been killed or seriously injured. Even a trained stunt man, accustomed to diving from great heights, would not have been able to pull it off, much less those poor, frantic women.

Of the four people who jumped or fell on that ghastly afternoon, one lived. Natalie Smith, a thirty-nine-year-old woman whose husband had been paralyzed for years, was rushed to Charity Hospital, a pulplike bundle of blood and twisted flesh and bones. She, too, fell nine stories from the beauty shop to an adjacent roof. No one thought that she had a chance to survive. Except her. After months in the hospital, she was back home, pushing her crippled husband in his wheelchair.

She later told me from her bed in Charity Hospital, "As I lay here, mangled and broken, I could easily give up. But then I think of my husband; and the will to live, the desire to *make it*, floods my whole being. Who would take care of *him*? Who would bathe and dress and feed him? There is no one but me. So I *tell* the Lord that I am going to get well. And I will."

When the smoke finally cleared and the last engine left the scene of the burned and charred Rault Center, the tragic total was: four dead; five seriously injured; plus many firefighters hurt or overcome. But what we cannot tally, the figure that cannot be put in an adding machine, was the terrible pangs of sorrow; the deep grief; the terrible torment; the sights and sounds of that day that left scars on the hearts and lives of every firefighter there.

When the elevators had stopped, Capt. Richard Labrusa was leading a group of men that had walked up the fifteen stories carrying hoses, respirator packs, and heavy equipment. He remembers too vividly, "We could hear them screaming in the beauty shop; we could hear them through the wall. We could hear each terrible explosion— and we couldn't get to them."

And weary firemen, sick at heart, plunged in grief, each

87

blackened and scorched, returned to their station houses that evening and began to shower and scrub clean. But as each man looked back over those unforgettable hours, there were scars left that would never heal; memories that could never be scrubbed away. These brave men's hearts were full of compassion and sorrow for those unknown, yet very real victims.

"We did everything possible that we could."

The firefighters went far beyond their call of duty; but still the scars were etched deep, deep—forever.

As I eased Car 30 into the carport of the rectory, Fran, my secretary, met me with concern in her eyes.

"Father, there's about twenty calls that you have to return. But maybe you should take this one first. It's a fireman whose wife wants to divorce him! She claims he loves his job more than her."

CHAPTER 10

Bananas Foster Hot, Bananas Foster Cold

9:15 P.M.

GLORIA AND MIKE HANEY are friends of mine from Indianapolis, and recently they were visiting New Orleans for a few days. After the Saturday evening mass and novena to St. Jude, they wanted to dine at Brennan's on Royal Street.

The food was superb, and we crowned a delightful evening by ordering Brennan's famous Bananas Foster.

José, the waiter, was doing his magic with the fire and all the ingredients, when Buzzy, the maitre d', came up behind me and whispered, "There's some trouble in front, Father. A woman is hysterical out in the foyer. I hate to disturb you, but could you come and talk to her?"

I cast a soulful eye on the luscious bananas about to be cooked in a rich liqueur sauce and told my friends to go ahead with the dessert. I would be right back, I assured them; or at least as soon as I could.

A middle-aged, extremely well-dressed woman and her husband were trying to tell two plainsclothesmen what had happened. The more the woman talked, the more shrill and hysterical she became. "And it happened right there—across the street! Right on Royal Street!" And she pointed across the street to the spot.

Royal and Bourbon are the two main streets of New Orleans' world-famous French Quarter and are usually thickly populated in the evenings with nightclubbers and diners and shoppers promenading and enjoying the excitement.

"There were three of them," the woman panted. "Two got alongside me, and the other stopped my husband to ask directions. First thing I knew one of them had a pistol at my head! At my *head!*" And she demonstrated where the gun was placed, using her right forefinger and thumb.

"Could you give us a description, please?" asked one of the detectives.

"—then before I knew it, one of the others had grabbed my purse."

"Were they white or black? What did any one of them look like? What were they wearing?" repeated Joe Taylor, who wanted to get a description out on the air as soon as possible.

"When he got the purse, he yelled to the others, 'Let's go!' And then before he ran, he pulled the trigger of the gun at my head! . . . There was a click; thank God it didn't go off. And he laughed and ran. Please get him!" And the woman broke down again in sobs.

"Which direction did they run in?" asked Joe.

"That next street down—whatever it is. We're from Atlanta and don't know these names." She was trembling violently now, as the realization dawned on her of how close she had come to death.

I asked Buzzy to phone her hotel, the Monteleone, and have the house doctor meet her and administer some sedation. I told him that I would drive her over there in a few moments. Buzzy nodded and left.

"Three white males—approximately how old?" Taylor continued.

"All about twenty-five or so," the husband interjected. "The one with the pistol had a white cowboy or Stetson hat on. Instead of asking us all these silly questions, why don't you get out after them? They can't be far away; it just happened five minutes ago!"

The detectives stopped their writing and looked at him. New Orleans police—and police all over the country—have learned that it's often better to let their eyes, not their lips, give messages. Det. Pete Reynolds, Taylor's partner, finally broke the silence.

"Sir, we need as good a description as possible so that our men in the streets will have something more definite to go on."

And as the husband, pale and trembling, tried to supply a more complete description, I drove Mrs. Thomas Alberts of Atlanta, Georgia, over to the Monteleone Hotel where the doctor was waiting to treat her for shock, nerves, and hysteria. I asked her if she wanted me to phone any of her family in Atlanta. She said no, she didn't want to worry them. Telling her I'd contact her if anything happened, I said good night.

Driving back to Brennan's on Royal Street I flipped on Channel 1. A voice suddenly broke in:

"Car 304. We're trying to follow a red and white Chevy—looked like a '72 or '73—going at a high rate of speed; possibly coming from the French Quarter. Three subjects in the car—looked like one was wearing a cowboy hat."

DISPATCHER: "You got him in sight, 304?"

CAR 304: "No, by the time we turned around, we lost him. We're playing the area now. Any further description on the other two dudes?"

And so began The Chase. The Chase is undoubtedly one of the most exciting moments in police work. And often enough, the dangers, the speeds, the risks to policemen's lives are unknown and unappreciated by the public.

DISPATCHER: "Attention all units. Looking for three

white males, about twenty-five to twenty-eight years old. Two have sandy hair; average height, whatever *that* is. One wore a brown jacket; the other a red pullover sweater. Third subject had a cowboy hat, white shirt, and Levis—should be in possession of $312 in American currency and various credit cards in an alligator purse. Last seen on foot running from Royal down Iberville towards Rampart. Use caution—at least one of them is armed with a snub-nosed, silver automatic. End of description."

CAR 107: "What are they wanted for?"

DISPATCHER: "A 65–P and possible 27–30." [Purse-snatching and attempted murder.]

There followed some routine police talk for a few moments on other calls, then an excited 304 again broke in:

CAR 304: "This is 304. We see them again now, going at a high rate of speed lakebound on Elysian Fields. They've turned left on Mirabeau."

DISPATCHER: "Where are you, 304?"

CAR 304: "At Elysian Fields and Lombard. We're about four or five blocks behind them—they must be doing seventy-five miles an hour."

CAR 707: "Car 707 to Headquarters—I—"

DISPATCHER: "All units: *Keep the air clear.* We're working a chase on Channel 1. If you've got an emergency, go on Channel 4. Any units around Elysian Fields, come in."

CAR 311: "311's going."

DISPATCHER: "10–04."

CAR 315: "315's rolling."

DISPATCHER: "That's 10–04."

CAR 320: "320's going."

DISPATCHER: "10–04, sir."

CAR 320: "Anything new on the description?"

DISPATCHER: "Same thing, Sergeant. Three white males, possibly in a red Chevy with a white vinyl top. One of the subjects is wearing a white or light-colored cowboy hat—304 spotted them turning west on Mirabeau from Elysian Fields."

CAR 701: "Permission for a 10–40, please?"

DISPATCHER (annoyed): "Asked you to keep the air clear, sir. We're working a chase!"

CAR 701 (sheepishly): "10–04."

CAR 304 (excited): "Their car's turned over. They're running—three of them at the corner of Mirabeau and Warrington Drive. They're heading into some bushes."

DISPATCHER (calmly): "Repeat the address, 304."

A long moment of silence—then:

CAR 304 (panting): "Me and my partner's going around the block on foot. There's a couple of houses near the end of this area. Tell the units to come to the 4800 block of Warrington."

DISPATCHER: "That's 10–04. 312, you take the other side by Allan and Brutus."

CAR 312: "We're 10–97, sir. Getting out—"

CAR 320: "I'm just about 10–97 on Warrington."

CAR 304: (excited): "Just heard shots fired!"

DISPATCHER: "From where, 304?"

Two voices were heard, talking over each other.

DISPATCHER (calmly): "Too many units—one at a time."

CAR 30: "Car 30's rolling." And I wheeled my new Ford from Royal and St. Louis out toward Elysian Fields. Bananas Foster were completely forgotten.

DISPATCHER: "That's 10–04, Car 30."

The excitement of The Chase mounts. The Chase: one or more criminals trying at all costs, trying desperately, taking every chance and every gamble to elude and outwit the law. The Chase has to be handled intelligently and skillfully; with deliberation; with care. Often the pursued—the criminals—have police radios and are monitoring every word the police utter and know exactly where the web is tightening.

93

I secretly wondered, as I neared Elysian Fields and the action, whether the Atlanta couple, safely back in their hotel room on Royal Street, appreciated all this manpower and effort—for their alligator purse!

CAR 304 (shouting): "304! Two more shots—from back in the woods!"

DISPATCHER: "Location, 304?"

CAR 304: "Somewhere between Mirabeau, Brutus, Warrington, and Allen."

DISPATCHER: "311 is in there someplace. Use caution. 316, take Brutus. Possibly they're over there now."

CAR 316: "10–04, sir."

CAR 320: "Get some more units out here."

DISPATCHER: "No more Third District units available, sir. Any available units in other districts, come in."

CAR 702: "702. Want me to roll?"

DISPATCHER: "Check with your rank. Let me know."

CAR 702: "10–04, sir."

DISPATCHER: "Come in, 304. What is your location?"

No answer.

CAR 702: "I'm rolling, sir."

DISPATCHER: "10–04—go into the area of Mirabeau and Brutus. Check with 320."

CAR 304 (panting; shouting): "They're—back—here. Just [panting] saw two of them split up. Don't know where the third one is."

DISPATCHER: "Where are you, 304?"

CAR 304 (out of breath): "My partner's gone down the alley behind the 4800 block—Warrington [panting]. I'm on the side of the corner house—Warrington and Brutus."

DISPATCHER: "Use caution—at least one of them's armed."

CAR 304: "Well aware of that, sir. They just fired three shots at my partner."

DISPATCHER: "That's 10–04."

CAR 320: "320 to Headquarters—get a K-9 unit out here!"

DISPATCHER: "Headquarters to any K-9 unit!"

EMERGENCY UNIT 852: "We'll roll over there."

DISPATCHER: "That's 10–04, 852."

CAR 30: "Car 30's 10–97."

DISPATCHER: "10–04, Father."

CAR 706: "706 is rolling, with permission of 720."

DISPATCHER: "10–04—any K-9 unit—come in."

CAR 304 (panting; shouting): "One's under the house!"

DISPATCHER: "Location, 304?"

CAR 304: "4893 Warrington."

CAR 320: "Wait for the K-9 unit, 304. Where's the other one?"

CAR 304: "My partner says one of them's still in the bush someplace."

CAR 320: "Use caution, 304. 307 and 311 are on foot, coming in from the other side."

K-9 UNIT: "K-9 to Headquarters—looking for us?"

DISPATCHER (calmly): "That's 10-04—you're wanted at 4800 Warrington Drive. Suspect under the house. Make it on a Code 3."

K-9: "10-04, sir."

And so Patrolman Ron Dumas with his partner, a black German shepherd named Chief, headed for the scene. By now, under the command of Car 320 (Sgt. Tim Mueller), Cars 304, 305, 307, 311, 316, 702, and 706, plus two detective units, with 852 (the emergency unit) and Car 30 (the chaplain) standing by, had all spread out around the area like a giant, deadly fishnet, waiting for Chief to come and point out the prey in the dark of a moonless New Orleans night.

When Officer Dumas arrived with his dog nine minutes later, The Chase continued. I stayed with the sergeant and watched the small army in blue as they tightened the net.

Chief, barking and straining at the leash, was delighted to be in action. He approached the opening under the house and, growling, awaited further commands from his master. After a few moments I heard:

K-9: "K-9 to 320."

CAR 320: "Yeah, K-9?"

K-9: "We've got one of 'em under the residence. He's comin' out."

CAR 307: "This is 307. We're on the other side of the house now."

CAR 316: "I'm right behind you, K-9."

In a matter of minutes, which seemed much, much longer, a suspect in a red, pullover sweater emerged from under the house, hands bleeding and clothing torn. He looked fearfully at the snarling Chief and muttered, "O.K. Keep that damn animal away from me. I wanna call my lawyer. I'm gonna sue every one of you! I didn't do nothin'—"

As the men from Car 316 snapped handcuffs on him and searched him thoroughly, Sergeant Mueller asked, "Where are your two buddies—especially the cowboy?"

"What buddies? I was just walkin' around the neighborhood."

"Tom, put him in the back of your car till we scoop up his pals."

Patrolman Tom Orsino (316) was getting name, address, and other information from the suspect's license when Headquarters called the sergeant.

CAR 320: "This is 320."

DISPATCHER: "We just ran a check on that overturned car involved in the chase. It was stolen this morning from the Marriott Hotel parking lot—registered to a J. B. Owens, Luling, Louisiana. Two-door Chevy; red body, white vinyl top. License: 103-L-916—10-04 on that?"

CAR 320: "That's 10-04 and thank you. Send a tow truck

to Mirabeau and Warrington and have the car brought to Headquarters."

DISPATCHER: "10-04, sir. Headquarters to 4219 . . ."

TRUCK 4219: "4219."

DISPATCHER: "You're needed over at Mirabeau and Warrington. Overturned stolen car—10-04?"

TRUCK 4219: "That's a 10-04, sir."

Meanwhile, Chief, Dumas, and about twelve uniformed officers and three or four plainclothesmen from Maj. Henry Morris' crack detective bureau were carefully closing the ring where an armed, dangerous man lurked, possibly ready to kill.

They found him fifteen minutes later. He had covered himself with leaves and was half-buried in the soft mud. Chief was there, however, and the flight and The Chase were over. As the man stood up, with hands raised, one of the officers plopped a muddy and crushed white cowboy hat, found nearby, on his head.

"Here's your hat, cowboy. Where's your other friend? And the gun?"

"Gun? What gun? What's this all about?"

Handcuffs snapped his hands securely behind his back, and he was thoroughly frisked. He looked defiantly at the officers standing around him with drawn guns and spat viciously.

Sergeant Mueller said, "Take them both back to the victims at the Monteleone and get a positive identification. Then book 'em on four counts: attempted murder of a policeman, auto theft, attempted murder of Mrs. Alberts, and purse snatching!"

"No weapons on him, Sarge," one of the officers said, "but there's exactly three hundred and twelve bucks in his pocket. Isn't that a coincidence?"

Mueller nodded. "Probably find the gun and the purse later—in the morning, I'd guess. You O.K., Bob?"

"Yeah, he's a lousy shot. Or thank God there's no moon. Me and my partner need a uniform change, though!"

Eight policemen and Chief spent the next hour and a half combing every inch of that dark area, while others searched each of the four houses in the block—all to no avail. Somewhere, somehow, the third suspect had slipped away.

I drove back to the Monteleone Hotel, where Mr. and Mrs. Thomas Alberts of Atlanta were asked to come down to the lobby. The lady had made a remarkable comeback. She appeared cool, healthy—composed and disdainful.

And I then looked at the four officers who had crawled through underbrush and barbed wire, who had faced gunfire from a dangerous man, who had looked at death out there in the dark. Their uniforms were torn; their faces grimy. But they—and the entire team—had done the job. My heart beat a bit faster and I'm sure my eyes conveyed the pride, as they had so many times, in the men of the New Orleans Police Department.

After Mr. and Mrs. Alberts positively identified the two men sitting in the cage of the patrol car and promised to come down to Headquarters in the morning, they turned and made their way back to the elevators. I caught up with them and was just about to ask how they were feeling and bid them a pleasant good evening, when I heard her snap, "You know, Thomas, I heard things about this police department. It certainly took them long enough, didn't it? And did you see how dirty they looked?"

I turned away in sad disbelief and headed back to some very cold—and sour—bananas.

CHAPTER 11

The Cop Who Went Bad

THE MAN, DRESSED IN FADED BLUE-JEANS and white T-shirt, eased up the stairs. Slowly, quietly, without a sound—just like they taught him—he approached the second-story apartment along the balcony. He flattened his lean body against the wall, moved very slowly, and listened. His trained ear caught the sounds of laughter and a stereo playing softly inside. And he clenched his teeth when he heard the intimate whisperings and the tinkling of ice in glasses.

The man slipped his hand under his shirt and drew an automatic from his belt. It might have been sixty minutes that passed; it might have been sixty seconds. He never knew.

Suddenly in a mad, impetuous moment of anger and fury and desperation, he sprang to the door and with a powerful kick, almost tore it from its hinges. With a pantherlike motion, he was in the room, both hands holding the automatic pointed at the nude couple. His feverish eyes saw the paraphernalia—the "cooker," the fixings—on a small table nearby. He saw the syringe on the night table, and his mind went sick and blank.

The man in the bed saw him first.

"No, Phil, no—for God's sake. Let me exp—"

Two shots tore his stomach out, and he rolled from the bed, eyes glazed, blood spurting from his naked belly and chest. The young woman screamed and drew a robe around her and began to sob.

"I didn't mean it, Phil—I didn't! He made me do it; he made—"

"Shut up, slut!" Phil spat through clenched teeth. "You loved me so much, didn't you! You were the one that played me for a sucker; pretended that you and I would make it for the rest of our lives. You *bitch!*"

He paused for a moment and then continued in a quiet, changed voice.

"Yeah— God, what an ass I was. A whole career ahead of me; best record in my district; up for sergeant—till I met *you*. God!" He sank in the chair near the bed, keeping the revolver pointed at the trembling, sobbing woman. "Yeah—look at Police Officer Philip Espositto now. Look at a broken-down bum, a junkie who betrayed everything he stood for by knocking down addicts on the street for the stuff—stuff that I hate now with everything I got inside me." And he kicked the table containing the narcotics paraphernalia across the room.

His eyes were blurred; the room began to swirl. And then he heard those terrible words, spoken with a new hatred and venom, coming from the scornful lips of the woman.

"Loved *you*? You damned fool. You just shot the man I loved. You were just useful to us—as a cop. Stupid sucker!"

Phil put his hand to his eyes and stumbled toward the door. "Just leave me alone, Gail. I came by to pick up my TV set. Just get out of my life."

"Leave you alone?" she screamed. "I'm going to see you in hell! You just killed the man whose baby I'm carrying!"

"Ba—baby?"

A loud explosion started somewhere in the back of his head and zoomed around from back to front—front to back—looking for a way out. It was like a demonic roman candle. And then it exploded.

And when it exploded, Phil pointed the gun at the woman and pulled the trigger.

Father Nick is one of my closest friends. He had been my superior in the seminary through the years of philosophy and theology and later was named provincial of the Oblate Southern Province for six years. The popular priest had also later served as pastor of the St. Louis Cathedral in New Orleans when I arrived here and was a big help to me in getting started, in getting to know the ropes. Now semi-retired, Father Nick comes to St. Jude to help out during the three yearly Solemn Novenas.

It was 1:30 P.M., and we were just finishing lunch. It was the third day of the Solemn Novena, and six of us Oblates were sitting around the table, chatting, laughing, relaxing, reminiscing.

Teresa, the receptionist, buzzed the dining room and Father Nick answered. "It's for you, Pete."

I dropped my napkin on the table and took the receiver. "Hello?"

There was a long silence on the other end, and I repeated the hello. Finally, a tight, strained voice said. "I hear you're a pretty straight guy."

"I try to be. Who's this, man?"

"Never mind that now. I've just killed two people. What do you think of that?"

"I think I'd like to talk to you."

"And turn me in?"

Before I could say a word, the voice continued. "Stay by the phone. Don't tell anyone I called. I'll call you again in thirty minutes."

The phone went dead.

I immediately dialed Headquarters. "Command Desk, please." After a few moments the commander of the watch, Sergeant Schick, answered.

"Yeah, Padre, what can we do for you?"

"Anything special happening in the streets?"

"Naw—just about the usual."

"Any shootings or 30's?"

"Oh, yeah. Matter of fact, Homicide's over there now—on Decatur Street—1108. Looks like a junkie love nest. One man is dead; they brought the woman to Charity."

"She dead?"

"Not yet, but she don't look too good."

"Any suspects on that?"

"Not yet."

"O.K.—and thanks."

I looked at my watch. In another ten minutes the mystery caller would—maybe—be dialing again. I called a priest at the St. Louis Cathedral and asked him to go over to the Decatur Street address and attend a man who had just been shot.

At 2:30 P.M., the phone rang again—on Line 2, the chaplain's hot line.

"Still there?"

"Sure am, man. Look, why don't you give me a name? Hate to be calling you 'man' all the time."

The phone went dead again. I mentally kicked myself for blowing it and vowed not to try any more funny lines.

The radio was softly playing "Stranger on the Shore," and I was sitting alone in the office now, rosary in hand, when the phone rang again. Line 2. It was Headquarters.

"Hey, Father; on that 30 that I told you about a while ago—we have a suspect."

My heart began to pound.

"Who?"

"I hate to tell you this, but it looks like it was one of ours—a cop. Guy in the Ninth District—Phil Espositto. He was a friend of the broad who was shot. When she regained consciousness at the hospital, she told all. She still may die. Incidentally, she was a few months pregnant. And the baby is still alive—barely."

"God!" I muttered. Now it began to make sense. The young policeman, scared as hell, was running, hiding, frantically phoning the chaplain for help. And I felt totally powerless.

Sergeant Schick continued, "We've got all men possible looking for him. The gal, Gail Simpson, said that he'd never be taken alive; that he'd shoot the whole department first and anyone who came near him. We believe he's heavily armed.

"His father lives across the river—we've got his house staked out now; but we don't think he's dumb enough to go there. Strange thing, Padre, he was a damned good cop."

After Headquarters hung up, I again waited—and continued to pray.

I called the receptionist on the intercom.

"Teresa, keep Line 2 open. Don't let anyone use it. If it rings, I'll answer it."

I sat and stared at the wall and thought about a scared, frightened, and angry young man, zigzagging across the city, eyes probably glued on the rearview mirror. Or maybe he was hiding out in a movie. Or maybe he was catching a bus. Maybe, maybe, maybe. If only I could talk to him.

Line 2 rang with a harsh jangle.

"I'm running, but I'm telling you—they're not going to take me."

"Phil?" I spoke in a quiet, almost conspiratorial voice.

"You know?"

"Yeah, I know. Listen, let me come see you. Tell me where you are. I'll—"

The phone went dead.

Jeez, I blew it again! I thought.

The theology books, with their thousands of cases, never had one like this. The rosary moved through my fingers, and I prayed with every ounce of energy I had. "Saint Jude, help of the hopeless, pray for him, help him. Help me help him—"

There was no call during the next half hour. I kept picking up Line 2 to make sure that it was clear; that it was working. Other phone calls came in for me; Teresa diverted them to Father Nick or one of the other priests in the house. The hour came for the 3:30 P.M. novena, and I was scheduled to lead the novena prayers, which follow the speaker's homily. I called upstairs to Father Quinlivan and asked him to handle the service; I was working a Signal Red.

At 4:00 P.M. the phone rang again.

"Did you tell them that I've been calling?"

"Not a word, Phil. You can believe that."

"Why can I believe that?"

"Because I told you—and because I'm straight. Like you said."

"O.K. Now listen to me. Can you come out to the Lakeside Shopping Plaza?"

"Of course."

"Go in Marty's Donut and Coffee Shop. Sit at the counter, and I'll meet you. We'll go out to my car; they know yours too good. Got it?"

"Sounds good, Phil. I'll be there in about twenty minutes. And listen—hang in there; I want to help you."

"You *want* to—but *can* you?"

And the phone hummed dead again.

Lakeside Plaza is a huge compound of department stores, shops, theatres, and restaurants sprawling in the middle of about ten acres of parking area, not too far from beautiful Lake Pontchartrain. Twenty minutes later, I was cruising slowly around the parking lot, dodging other drivers intent at all costs on capturing a parking space. My eyes followed every shop in the huge octagonal mart: Ted's

Shoes; Crescent Liquors; Dolly's Dolls; the Pink Poodle Beauty Shoppe; the Sparkle Jewelry Store; D. H. Holmes' giant department store—and then around to the other side. More shops.

Lord, there must be ten thousand of them, I thought. A-2 Television Sales and Service; Lon's Po-Boy; Cinderella Bras and Girdles . . .

"Marty's, where *are* you?" And then I saw it.

Parking in the middle of a cluster of cars, I walked into the shop, sat at the counter, and ordered coffee. I had just added the sugar when a voice behind me whispered, "Follow me, Padre. Stay a bit behind me. I'll meet you in my car."

I dropped a quarter on the counter and followed him out. As I climbed into the front seat of a blue Duster, I whispered a tiny prayer for the right words. God, he looks young, I thought.

The man looked at me for a long time, and I held his gaze.

"See this?" With a swift motion Phil yanked away a sweater which had been covering something in the back seat of the Duster. I looked and saw two revolvers, a shotgun, and boxes of ammo. "And I've got this." He opened his jacket to show a .38 in his belt.

The young policeman put his head on the steering wheel and was silent for a long while. I waited for him to speak. And when he did, the story came out in painful, choked gasps.

It was a sad story of infatuation, lust, love, desire for a woman he thought he loved—and who he thought loved him.

"God, I'd have done *anything* for her, and I did. You know what I mean?"

As the story tumbled out, he mumbled, "She started me off on grass, and because we made it really great when we were on it, I began to try to get her the stuff. That was over a year ago. Then we went to amphetamines and pills and acid and everything, plus booze. Everything. I don't know how they didn't suspect something at work; but they didn't. I was a good cop; made lots of arrests—good arrests. You know what I mean? Finally, she told me that if I really loved her, we'd try H together. She had made a purchase. I didn't know it then, but she had been on heroin for over a year. Her and her friend."

He rolled up his jacket sleeve. "Look at this!" And I saw the ugly, telltale tracks on his arm. "I had a fix this morning, just before I went to the apartment, but it's wearing off now, and I really feel lousy."

A Jefferson Parish sheriff's car cruised by, and I closed my eyes and hoped that Phil hadn't seen it. But he had.

"You didn't tell anyone that you were meeting me, did you?"

"I swear to you that no one was told—and no one followed me. That JP unit is just prowling, looking for parking lot burglars and purse-snatchers."

Phil lay back and put his head on the back of the seat and closed his eyes. And he continued to talk in a low, slurred, barely audible voice.

Thirty-five minutes later, he stopped talking.

"Now you know everything about me and what a bastard I've been. I have a father who's sick—all this will kill him. I've lost my job. If I'm caught I'll get fifty years to life in Angola—maybe even the chair. Do you know what it means for a cop to get sent to the penitentiary? It's a death warrant. There are guys there who were sent up by me. No cop—no cop—can survive in jail. There's only one way out: to run."

"Phil, I've listened to you for almost an hour; now will you listen to me?"

The young man turned and looked directly in my eyes.

He seemed to be searching for even a glimmer of hope—
one tiny shred of a chance. His narcotic-blurred eyes tried
to focus clearly on me, the only hope he had.

"First of all, you didn't kill the woman. Gail is still very
much alive. That's how the police know it was you—she
told them. Second, if you tell in court exactly what you told
me just now—the whole story—you might not even get to
Angola; they might give you some time at DeQuincy [min-
imum security prison for first offenders]. And I promise
you that whatever happens, I'll be with you all the way."

"Why?"

"Because I believe in you—and God does, too. You're
young. You've got a lot of living—good living—yet to do in
this life. Close the door on what happened yesterday and
today. It can be a whole new ball game. It's not how you
begin this life that counts most, Phil, it's how you *finish*
it."

After a long pause, I continued. "Remember Judas, who
betrayed Jesus? He began life very well—was an apostle,
in fact—and ended at the end of a rope, a betrayer. Saint
Peter began real bad—by denying Christ—but ended up
darned good."

Phil was looking at me—but was he *seeing* me? He was
hearing me—but was he *listening* to me? Or was he
seeing and listening to a very desirable woman to whom
he might someday return and take up where he had left
off?

"And, third, if you decide to run, you'll probably be dead
or in Parish Prison by ten o'clock tonight. They've got a lot
of people looking for you."

I pressed on. Earnestly.

"Phil, the press is being kept out of it. It won't be in the
newspapers or on radio or TV. I'll get to your father later
and explain a lot of things to him. I can reassure him. I
can give him hope that one day, and maybe a day not too

far in the future, this whole lousy nightmare will be behind you. But the point is, Phil, *I believe in you.* And I promise that I'll stick with you."

The man rested his head again on the steering wheel for such a long while that I thought he was asleep. A long silence followed—maybe fifteen minutes.

Children were laughing not far away; lovers were walking into the movie theatre; an occasional car horn would blow; someone's radio was softly playing from a nearby car. Everything was perfectly normal, except that sitting beside me was a heavily armed, desperate, half-drugged, frightened man—debating whether to live or not.

After what seemed an eternity, Phil reached into the back seat, lifted the small arsenal and put it on his lap. It was getting dark now, and in the failing light I could see the young man's eyes, filled with tears, as he stared into nothingness. Finally, he whispered to me, so softly that I could hardly hear the words.

"I'll give myself up to you on one condition."

"What's that, Phil?"

"That you first take me to the hospital to see Gail."

"I'll have to make a phone call on that."

"O.K.—but if they say no, you'll never see me again— alive."

"I'll try, Phil."

As I got out of the car, stiff from two hours of sweating and sitting, Phil reached out his hand. "I trust you, Father Rogers. Don't let me down."

I looked him in the eyes again and nodded my head.

In a nearby phone booth, my nickel dropped in place, and soon a voice at Homicide answered.

"Who's working the Espositto case? This is Father Rogers."

"This is Pritchard. Got any information?"

"Yeah, maybe. Lieutenant McNabb there?"

"At the hospital. What can you tell me?"

"If I brought Phil Espositto down to Charity Hospital, could I take him up to see Gail—the girl friend—if he'd then surrender himself?"

The police officer shouted. "You got him? Where?"

"You didn't answer the question, Mr. Pritchard."

"As far as I'm concerned there'd be no deals. But—"

"I'll try the hospital and see if I can get the lieutenant."

"Wait, you can't—" And he was listening to a dead phone.

I ran back to the car hoping that Phil would still be there. He was. I told him that I was going to speak to McNabb who was in charge of the case.

Phil mumbled, "Better hurry up. I think I'm changing my mind."

Back in the phone booth, it seemed forever before I heard the words, "Lieutenant McNabb here."

"Lieutenant?—Father Rogers." And I briefed the veteran detective on what was taking place.

"Where are you now?"

"I'd rather not say, Lieutenant, but my God, this is important. The man is going to wipe himself out and maybe some of our people, if we don't go along with him. He just wants to see her for five minutes, then he'll surrender to you. I'll have his weapons. My Lord, why the hesitation?"

" 'Cause he might use you as a hostage."

"He won't."

"How do you know, Father?"

"Because I believe in him, Bob."

There was a long pause while the detective sized up all the possibilities. Finally he said, "O.K. Bring him in. I'll see that he gets a few moments with her. She's fully conscious now; they're going to take out the bullet in the morning. But only for a few minutes."

"Five."

"O.K. Five. Be careful, Padre."

I returned to the car and breathed easier when I saw Phil still sitting there—staring out at nothing. We locked the Duster, leaving it where it was, and Phil gave me the keys.

"I won't be needing these for a while."

"I hope not too long a while, Phil. I'll get the car over to your father's house tomorrow. It'll be O.K. parked here tonight."

For the first time during this long and harrowing day, a trace of a smile appeared on Phil's lips. "I dunno, Padre. There's a lot of crime going on these days."

At 8:34 in the evening, Car 30 came to a stop near the emergency ramp at Charity Hospital. I put all Phil's guns and shells under the front seat and covered the rest of the stuff on the back floor. We had just hit the sidewalk when McNabb and four of his men were around us. "Hi, Father! Hi, Phil."

"I'm not walking in with you—just with the priest."

I gave the lieutenant the keys to my car. "Phil's things are under the front seat and on the back floor. We'll see you in five minutes."

She was in Ward 504 East. There was a policewoman near her bed and three or four plainclothesmen talking at the door of the ward. McNabb and one of his men followed us at a distance, silent and watchful, but Phil's eyes were only on one person—the woman whom he thought he loved.

He went over to the bed and knelt down beside her. "Gail, I just had to come and tell you that I'm sorry and that I'm going to give myself up. Wait for me, and one day we'll begin a whole new life over again—a new way; the right way—the straight way. What do you say?"

She opened her eyes and looked at him.

"Come a little closer," she whispered.

With a glimmer of hope in his eyes, Phil moved closer to her. She raised herself a little, and then with all the hatred and venom she possessed, she spat in his face.

"I hate you," she hissed. And turning her face away, she said to the police, "Get him out of here!"

The nonjury trial was a quiet one. Strangely enough, there was no publicity; no TV cameras; no screaming radio bulletins or headlines about the cop who "went bad." I offered to testify about my belief in the man but was not called during the trial.

I sat in with lawyers and assistant DA's and listened as the charges were reduced to manslaughter—a lesser crime than first or second degree murder. It was brought out at the trial how Phil was incapable of being totally responsible for his actions because of a large dosage of drugs in his system, which were both directly and indirectly caused by his association with one of the victims. His passion for the woman was also thrown on the table. The dead man's past was looked at. Phil's five years in the police department, with his brilliant record, without a blemish or even a complaint against him, was produced. Testimony by fellow officers told of his honesty and the quality of his arrests.

On the day before Phil Espositto was to be sentenced, I met with the judge in his chambers and went over the entire case from my point of view. He had been found guilty of manslaughter. The man admitted that he had committed the crime under the influence of drugs. He *was* an addict—but there was so much more.

The judge listened politely, said he would consider all the evidence, and only the evidence, and bade me goodbye.

The next day the sentence was handed down to Phil Espositto: ten years at hard labor in Angola Penitentiary!

CHAPTER 12

Jesus Was Double-Parked

6:30 A.M.

SOMETHING THAT IS ESPECIALLY PUZZLING to the general public is the often unasked, but frequently thought-of, question: "What do priests *do* all week?"

Hollywood has given the Catholic priest a very special niche.

The flicks have awarded us the all-time, all-American Oscar for Dullness. And it has been decreed that the priestly mold in which we are cast must never change. Hollywood has its idea of what a priest should look like, act like, wear, and how he should perform. Directors have set the solemn tones of his voice, his soulful (almost painful) expression. And these sacerdotal "musts" have been handed down from generation to generation of movie-maker and TV producer.

With a few notable exceptions, the films (that is, the writers, directors, and producers) have done quite a job portraying most things that a priest is *not*. Their caricature of the cleric and his duties is sometimes nothing less than ludicrous. And if we had a union, we would protest.

In the movies, the priest is usually a balding, obese, elderly man, slightly stooped, garbed in something out of the 1500s, whose one and only answer to every problem and crisis is uttered with a white-knuckled, sorrowful fervor, as he turns away: "God bless you, my son."

I've been a priest for twenty-seven years and have never—no, not once—gripped my hands tight, ground my teeth, and wheezed, "God bless you, my son!", much less turned away!

No one gets a bigger kick out of this comic-strip portrayal than the priests themselves, most of whom, incidentally, have a pretty good sense of humor.

Hollywood has all the ingredients to produce one of the most powerful dramas in the world, and they miss the boat. A story could—and maybe one day will—be written about the drama of the life of a Catholic priest, without white knuckles and rosary-rattling, but Hollywood is looking in all the wrong places. Or possibly it doesn't know *where* to look.

O.K. What *does* a priest do between the time he disappears from the altar after Sunday mass, until the next time the congregation sees him, walking toward that same altar, in the same vestments, ready to celebrate the Eucharist on the following Sunday?

Let's see. We're not only cheerleaders of the youth group; not only accountants; not only plumbers. We're not grim ascetics, found perpetually in a remote corner of the church, praying at all hours; we're not tough guys who hit fresh kids in the teeth (à la Spencer Tracy); we're not tea-sippers, gossiping and munching cookies daily with the ladies of the Altar Society; we're not great promotion men, putting up billboards telling about our next appearance in Madison Square Garden or the Cotton Bowl. And most of us are probably not great saints.

But we're trying. Trying to be all of these things—yet much, much more.

How does a priest spend his day? Well, let me describe our day, and then you might get some idea of how the "other six days" between Sundays are spent.

My daily routine usually begins around 6:30 in the morning, if I am slated for the early mass at 7:00 A.M.

Our downtown church is an extremely active place. The ministries here are divided into three major ones: the parish duties (the 1,000 apartments of the low-income Iberville Housing Project—about 5,000 people); the International Shrine of St. Jude, to which approximately 300,000 persons come yearly; and the police and fire ministries.

One of my facetious priest friends from Houston recently sat in the office and remarked, "Wow—what a job you've got! All you do is chase ambulances around day and night! Soft touch!" He was kidding, of course, but the police and firemen's coat and boots, hanging close to the front door, do emphasize a point. The fire coat is charred and worn now; the boots have trudged through many a fire scene, climbed many a ladder. Standing ready for action at any hour, they are the silent reminders that the pastor of this parish is also the pastor of another—the streets of New Orleans—and pastor of the men and women who patrol those streets to keep them as safe as possible.

Sam the mailman comes in at 9:00 A.M. on the dot with his cheery smile and big bag of mail. Following juice and New Orleans coffee in the rectory dining room and a glance at the sports page, we get to the mail. Since St. Jude's is a national shrine, the mail is heavy and some have laughingly dubbed us "the fifteen-cent theologians." A postage stamp, plus some prayer, time, and thought, enables us to write and answer many of the problems and crisis situations that arrive via Uncle Sam's postal routes.

Persons, many times anonymously, will open their hearts and souls to St. Jude via a letter. Persons with only a P.O. Box number will write—some on perfumed stationery, some on the kids' homework paper—and pour out their most intimate needs, their most pressing problems:

"Dear Father Rogers: I wanted to kill myself last night. Can I take a few moments of your time to tell you how I feel? No one, neither my husband nor my children, knows about this. . . ."

"Dear Father: My boyfriend and I got in this big hassle

the other day. He is pushing me to have an abortion, but I don't want . . ."

"Dear Omlette Fathers [He meant 'Oblate.']: I don write so good, but I hear you on the radio an I wanna tell you a big problem. I have a neybor who I think murdered his son . . ."

"Dear Father Rogers: The doctors gave up completely on my 5-year-old boy. He was struck by a car 2 weeks ago and has been in intensive care at Ochsner Hospital. I turned to St. Jude, and . . ."

"Dear Sir: I have 11 kids and no husband. They cut off my lights yesterday. Could you possibly send me . . ."

Fran, my secretary, pokes her head in the office door at ten minutes after ten and reminds me that next week's radio broadcast hasn't been done yet.

When I came to St. Jude in 1965, they were broadcasting over five radio stations. I silently thank the "saint of the impossible" who introduced me to Joe Costello. This genial genius, president of WRNO-FM, helped me streamline, tone up, and rearrange both the formula of our half-hour radio programs, as well as relocate and redecorate our St. Jude studio in the rectory. It was Costello who put the broadcast on its feet—or possibly its toes. It is now heard over twelve radio stations weekly in the Southeast. One of Joe's first suggestions was this piece of advice: "Father, instead of telling the sick persons that you've looked forward to coming into their *bedroom* this morning, just let it go that you're 'happy to come into their homes,' O.K.?" In addition to the radio ministry, we have also televised, for the past four years, the thrice-yearly Solemn Novena over WDSU-TV. This has been warmly received in homes, hospitals, and institutions for the elderly.

It's now 11:00 A.M., and back at the desk in my front office the buzzer sounds and more appointments come in: grieving wives with serious marriage problems; the painters looking for their money; a fireman who wants help in getting a transfer. One of our parishioners from the Project is in tears, asking us to get her son out of jail ("He didn't do it, fawdah; my boy was just sittin' in the car!").

There are men looking for work. A policeman has a gripe against his captain. Then there are sorrowing families arranging the time of a funeral tomorrow and a wake tonight; and happy families arranging for a wedding or a baptism. Parish Council President Chuck Hauschild enters and wants to go over the agenda for the council meeting Monday night. Young and dynamic Joe Canizaro, who recently donated to St. Jude the $200,000 building across the street, phones to see if I had gone over the plans for our proposed new St. Jude Center.

There is a staff of thirty dedicated lay people to be seen and helped and kept happy, and their weekly paychecks signed. The accountant enters and reminds me about some minor detail—like money. Then there are transients and beggars and drunks and con men—all wanting and waiting to "see the priest."

During all this, I have one ear tuned to the voice on the police radio that is going constantly. I listen for key signals. When I pick up one, all conversation in the office or on the phone ceases and full attention is given to the police or fire dispatcher.

The telephone rings day and night at Our Lady of Guadalupe rectory. Thank the good Lord, we have a dedicated corps of receptionists who take the many calls, complaints, questions, and demands to see or talk to one of the priests. They hear everything and learn to handle each caller kindly and efficiently, as callers who ask, for example, "Who is the patron saint of alcoholics?—you don't know? Well, why don't you look it up!" Or the receptionists listen to the most complicated case of spiritual direction. They deal with such subjects as the starting time and the amount of the "pots" for tonight's bingo, and note the address and location of a 20F (auto fatality) that the coroner's office is calling in. Recently, in one day alone, we logged over 250 telephone calls.

There is a special hot line for the use of police and fire departments and the coroner's office; it is not given to the general public. And when that line (Line 2) rings, it usually signifies something special—and another drama begins to unfold.

As in many other busy parishes, we have also installed a fourth line: "Dial St. Jude." This special line offers a "mini-meditation," usually lasting from sixty to ninety seconds. For a week at a time, each of us records these daily messages; over 150 persons daily phone in for that moment of "saying hello to the Lord."

One of the most important but sad facts about many church bulletins is that they are read by just about no one. To make our weekly bulletin a mite more attractive, we use all kinds of gimmicks—such as offering a set of St. Jude doubloons to the first person who phones in the spelling mistake that was purposely put in that week's bulletin. Or perhaps we'll try to recruit more volunteers by telling the "Round Tuit" story:

THE STORY OF THE ROUND TUIT

Tuits have been hard to come by, especially the round ones. But now, by special arrangement, yours is printed below. We rejoice with you because the demand has been great, and now that each family of the parish has one tuit, we expect many changes. Many problems will be solved, and Sunday attendance at mass should at least double now that each family has a round tuit available to them.

For you see, so many have said: "Father, I will come back to church just as soon as I can get a round tuit." Others have said: "I know I should come to Bible class; I know I should come to the youth club; I just never seem to get a round tuit." "I know I should be more involved in the life of the parish but I never seem to get a round tuit." Or: "I've been wanting to begin a program of tithing my income, or start singing in the choir, or teach CCD, but we've been so busy we just haven't gotten a round tuit."

Now *everyone* has his own "round tuit," and we know that great things are in store.

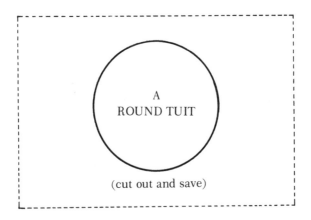

A
ROUND TUIT

(cut out and save)

Three times yearly—summer, fall, and winter—we con-duct the Solemn Novenas in honor of St. Jude. For the priests and staff, the work entailed is enormous: contact-ing and contracting a renowned speaker at least a year or two in advance; writing the promotional literature and the letters for over thirty thousand friends of St. Jude; pre-broadcasting the nine days of novena services, which are one half-hour each, or a total of eighty-one half-hour pro-grams; overseeing the decor and the decorations in the shrine, skillfully handled by artistic Irving Davis; hear-ing countless confessions during the novena services. Other details must be arranged: getting as much local parking space as possible; checking over the personnel for the free babysitting programs; looking over the music and the organists' schedules. These are but a few of the items that must be handled to insure a successful Solemn Novena.

The crowds attending these Solemn Novenas, renewals, are tremendous. About forty-five thousand people jam into the shrine for ten services daily over the nine days. And we have begun closed-circuit TV to accommodate the overflow crowds in our adjacent St. Jude Hall. The St. Jude novenas are a public display of faith and love rarely seen in our modern age.

But they take *work*.

The buzzer sounds again. Two policemen have a young white male in the outside office. Maria-Kay brings them in.

"This is the dude that knocked over your Saint Jude statue about a week ago," one of the officers explains. "We brought him then to the third floor of Charity (the psychiatric ward), and they cut him loose this morning. He's cleared. But we saw him going back into the church just now, so we brought him in here to talk to you."

"Why did you punch Saint Jude in the mouth?" I asked him.

The young man, Benny, looked at me with surprise. " 'Cause he wouldn't answer me."

I explained how the statue of St. Jude—and all the other statues in the shrine—were there merely to remind us of the saints' presence in heaven. I explained how we use statues to remind us that the saints are God's special friends. I added, "Just like I carry a photo of my mother in my wallet—just to remind me of what she looked like; of how pretty she was. But I don't expect her resemblance to talk back to me."

The police later turned Benny loose, telling him to stay away from St. Jude. And he promised them that he wouldn't slug him any more.

Once a week, each priest takes a day off. A day to get away from the crisis line; away from calls and pleas and cries for aid and help and assistance. A drive out into the beautiful Louisiana bayou country, a good meal, relaxing with friends, a movie, a round of golf or a hunting trip, a fishing sortie to reel in some of the Gulf of Mexico's famous redfish or trout: these are some of the ways that we priests relax and hope to return refreshed so that we can continue the never-ending job of bringing Christ to man by bringing man to Christ.

Then Fathers Roger Temme, ordained just two years, and James Miller, ordained over twenty years ago, troop into the office for our weekly clergy meeting. We schedule activities for the weeks ahead. We plan new ideas, new liturgies, new ways of bringing the youth and all the people to the Lord. There are many pluses that emerge from these important meetings.

At 12:00 noon every day there is another celebration of the Eucharist, and on Tuesdays and Thursdays, an additional third mass is added for the homeward-bound working people at 6:00 in the evening.

Each priest has direction of one of the many societies in the parish: the Legion of Mary; the Charismatic Prayer Group; the Youth Group (called the Jammers); the League of St. Jude, that loyal and dedicated group of women organized in 1966 by Antoinette Ancona and myself, which has done so much toward the restoration of the old and historical church. The League also built the new shrines of St. Jude as well as the Memorial Shrine to the Police and Firemen, and supports and maintains the St. Jude Baby Village. Other groups include the Inquiry Class, the Police and Firemen's Holy Name Society, the Parish Council, the Veteran Police Officers, and the Men of St.

Jude, with our so-necessary Wednesday evening bingos, presided over by President Joe Crespo. These are some of our groups and organizations, most of which have come into being over the last twelve years. The majority of our workers live outside the parish boundaries, but there are *no* boundaries to their love and zeal and devotion to the Shrine of St. Jude.

One day, as I was talking to Rita Forvendal and Millie Holiday, two of the officers of the League of St. Jude, Millie Brown, one of our receptionists, buzzed on the intercom. "You've *got* to see this, Father. At the front door."

A young man, about twenty-five years of age, stood there. "I'm Jesus," he stated, "and I need your help."

I looked at him. He had long, stringy blond hair and wore a brown burlap robe, tied at the waist with a piece of clothesline. He had sandals on his dusty feet, and around his neck he carried a live lamb.

"Jesus," I said, "it's nice to meet you—and your friend. Would you like a cup of coffee?"

"No," the vision serenely replied. "Just give me ten dollars, and I'll be off. I can't wait too long; I'm double-parked, and I don't want to get a ticket."

"Aw—they wouldn't give *you* a ticket, Jesus."

Jesus repeated his request for ten dollars.

I tried not to smile as I watched the lamb tinkle down the man's dirty collar.

"Can I see your car?" I ventured. He pointed to a gleaming 1977 Cadillac, parked double, in front of the rectory.

I explained that we would put him to work for a few hours at the going rate, and then he'd have enough to feed himself, his lamb, and to put some gas in the Caddy. His eyes blazed as he stormed off.

"Just wait—just wait till I tell my Mother on you!"

Following the noon mass, we priests at Guadalupe get together for a prayer session. Each of us takes a turn in selecting the Bible passages or leading the meditation, Divine Office, or shared prayer for that week. Following the prayer session, we sit down to lunch together.

The afternoons, following a short siesta, or rest period, are given to visiting: visiting the housing project, or one of the twenty-five hospitals in the area, or the firehouses and police stations, or the shut-ins. Visiting, we believe, is the heart of parish work.

Later, we prepare for the evening's meetings, banquets, talks, or appointments.

The phone calls continue, even during the night. It was early one Sunday, about 4:00 A.M., and I reached for the ringing phone. Sleepily, I greeted the caller.

"What time is your first mass?"

"Seven-thirty."

"What time is the next one?"

"Nine-thirty."

"And the third mass?"

"Eleven-thirty."

"Is that all you've got?"

"No, there's another one at seven-forty-five in the evening."

"Loralee," the man called to his companion, "they have church at seven-thirty, nine-thirty, and eleven."

"Eleven-thirty," I corrected.

"Eleven-thirty and seven-forty-five. Which one ya wanta go to?"

"The eleven—at the St. Louis Cathedral," she responded. "And get some more ice."

I sighed and wearily replaced the receiver.

In addition to these four Sunday liturgies, each with a St. Jude novena service, we have additional novena services at 2:00, 3:00, and 4:00 in the afternoon, and 6:30 and 7:30 in the evening, plus a Saturday vigil mass and novena service. It's a long, long day.

122

Every priest and minister is asked to give his share of invocations or blessings at banquets, dinners, anniversaries, weddings, graduations, rehearsal suppers, conventions, meetings, medical groups, political rallies, Carnival clubs, nurses' meetings, parades, and labor rallies—just to mention a few. But the police and fire chaplain gets even more than the usual share of invitations, and I reluctantly decline only if it is impossible for me to attend, because I always take a moment or two before the prayer to get in a "plug" for better working and pay conditions for our police and firemen.

On one occasion, I had given the blessing at the same hotel, in the same ballroom, for three consecutive daily luncheons. As I passed the headwaiter for the fourth day in a row, I quietly asked him, "Broiled chicken *again*, Gerhardt?"

He smiled. "No, Father," he said. "Today the *menu* has changed. How about the *prayer?*"

As night falls over the charming Crescent City, the action begins to pick up. Whether I am at meetings or dinners or seeing people in or out of the office, portable police radio Number 253 is chattering away in my back pocket, and I'm listening to Channel 1. The other police dispatchers know that, and if they need the chaplain, they will move over to Channel 1 and the familiar: "Car 30—Headquarters calling Car 30!" will be heard.

At about 12:30 A.M., I finally put the light out.

As I drift off to sleep, I know that my "other parishioners," the police and firemen, are not sleeping, but are alert and vigilant during the action-packed New Orleans night. And I know that they will call if they need me. My last prayer is a psalm for their safety, both physical and moral.

So life rolls on for the priests at St. Jude's, the downtown inner-city parish of New Orleans: bills to pay; sermons to write, prepare, and deliver; people who are, for one reason or another, upset with some one of us; children to direct toward our school, the Cathedral school on Dauphine Street. Daily advising, counseling, directing, helping, hoping. We keep our thumbs on the sometimes vibrant, sometimes weak, pulse of the people of God in New Orleans.

It is a beautiful life.

It is a life of service and action.

It is a life about which Hollywood, sadly, has no idea.

CHAPTER 13

Delta Towers Drama

5:15 P.M.

A LARGE CROWD HAD GATHERED ON THE STREET and near the doorways of the apartment-hotel called Delta Towers, on Canal and Claiborne, when I arrived on that sunny afternoon at 5:15. There were, I later found out, a thousand others watching the drama from office windows and apartments, and, in fact, one television station had sent up a crew to the top floor of a neighboring building to get it all on film.

It seemed that the whole world wanted to watch a man kill himself.

Suicides—or suicide attempts (called in police code "27–29–S")—are more popular with the masses than circuses, bingo games, or Mardi Gras parades. Suicides attract the attention, not only of the police and fire departments, but of the curious, the morbid, the innocent passerby, the blood-luster, the depressed, the tourist, the depraved.

As we were riding up to the eighteenth floor—the roof of the Delta Towers—I was briefed by Firefighter Richard Daley from the emergency squad, which is made up of the paramedics of our city. Daley's unit was standing by either to administer whatever medical aid might be necessary or to cover the remains with a sheet after the body had shattered on the street below. In the elevator, Richard told me that a young white male, about nineteen or twenty, was perilously perched on the ledge of the roof, with both legs over the side. There was nothing between him and the warm asphalt of Claiborne Street, eighteen floors below, except air. Other than that, no one knew anything about him.

Today's approach by firemen and policemen to suicides has changed quite a bit since the turn of the century. A story is told about a veteran cop back in 1925 who was called to the scene of a suicide attempt. The legendary policeman, looking at his watch, reportedly told the man, who was sitting in an open window contemplating a dive:

"Look, fella. It's six-forty-five. I get off at seven. By the time I cross this room and get to you, you either go out that window or, if you're still there, your ass goes to jail!"

The story may be apocryphal but it pointed up the kind of thinking that, in many instances, then prevailed in situations involving unfortunates bent on suicide.

And suicides occur all too frequently among police and firemen themselves. Many a cop has sat in my office and described the anguish of what it feels like to contemplate taking his life.

I remember one policeman whose wife had left him, taking their three kids with her. She had found out only a few weeks before about her husband's girlfriend, whom he had met five years previously at the Hummingbird Bar & Grill. Now the man was just completing fifteen days of a thirty-day suspension (WOP) for drinking on the job. During the wretched nights at home—alone, disheartened, looking at his children's picture—his gaze would drift to his .38, sitting in its holster on the chair. And he was tempted.

The national suicide rate for policemen is high—second only to doctors, according to reliable sources. Even policemen who apparently were in no trouble and who were having few problems at home have surprised everyone by killing themselves.

Now the elevator stopped on the roof, and I saw that a fence separated the man sitting on the ledge from a small army of newspapermen, photographers, police, firemen, bellboys, and hotel officials—all cajoling, threatening, entreating, or pleading with the youth not to jump.

Sgt. Mike Palmer was in charge and I asked him to please get everyone away from the fence and back to the doorway leading to the elevator. As always, the police were more than cooperative, and in a few minutes I was alone with the dark-haired man, whose face was turned away from me.

"Hi!" I called through the fence. "My name's Father Pete—they were a noisy bunch, weren't they?"

No response.

"You know, if you look the right way, you can see my little church from where you're sitting. Didja know that?"

He shifted slightly so that only one cheek of his rump was on the ledge and he could see from whom this new solitary voice was coming. Then he looked past me to the people in the hallway, now out of earshot.

"Don't come any closer, ya hear?" he said.

"I won't—I promise you. Can I talk to you for a minute?"

"Yeah." He drew heavily on a cigarette. "But it'll only *be* a minute."

I noticed that he was smoking Salems and that the pack in his shirt pocket seemed almost empty. Good. Even though I don't smoke cigarettes, there's always an extra package in the holy oil kit for moments like this.

"Boy—it's a gorgeous day. Look at that sky; not even a cloud."

"It's a lousy day."

"Why is it a lousy day?"

He shifted slightly, put both hands on the ledge on either side of him, and looked down—eighteen dizzying floors down, down, down—at the halted traffic, the people.

127

Slowly edging along the fence, I ventured, "Looks to me like you're either a painter or a construction worker."

Without looking my way, the good-looking young man said, "Right. How'd you guess?"

"Because most people couldn't look down the way you just did and not get dizzy. You must be used to heights. When I was in college I worked for Bethlehem Shipbuilding in Brooklyn."

"I work for Reynolds Construction. I mean I *did*—I got fired this morning."

"Is that Mike Reynolds? I know him real good."

"Yeah. Wasn't his fault, though. I was shittin' around all the time. This morning I showed up drunk again—but Mike's all right."

"Out drinking all night with the guys?"

"By myself."

"Why by yourself?"

"Same reason I'm up here by myself. Life ain't worth a shit. People ain't worth a shit. My wife ain't worth a shit."

"You're not up here by yourself."

He shifted again, threw me a look, and then, with a defiant gesture, flipped his cigarette down toward the waiting, jeering crowds below.

Good thing he can't hear them, I thought.

"And what's the problem with the wife?"

He fished out his pack of cigarettes, and I saw that I'd been right in thinking that his supply was running low—there were only two left. He lit one and then looked into the distance—way past the Mississippi River Bridge. "I dunno. It seems that there's a helluva *lot* wrong with her when we're in the house together or when we go out together—always findin' fault, always fightin', always fussin', always bitchin'. But from up here, she don't look so bad. Maybe *she* should be sittin' here."

He studied the end of the cigarette. "When I got home from work yesterday, there was a note—nice and neat. She said she was tired of all the fussin' and was going to leave. She's back at her mother's now, I guess." He paused a moment, then went on. "Things just seem to build up inside me—then something tears. Like when you put a gallon of water into a paper bag: the bag busts."

A fairly strong breeze blew in from the lake, and it began to get overcast and cloudy. I didn't like that. Sometimes the winds get mighty strong around New Orleans. I remembered a time not too long ago when I was talking to a man on top of the Mississippi River Bridge from which he was threatening to jump. Suddenly the winds came up, fast and strong, and almost blew the man and me from the spot where we were perched. And the water was two hundred feet below.

"What's your name, son?"

"Freddie Carson. What's yours?" And so began a dialogue between a distraught and depressed young man and a priest whose every word had to be the right one.

Twenty minutes went by, and he tossed the empty pack down on the people below.

"Here, try one of mine." I reached out to offer him a Winston.

"Stay where you are!" he shouted.

"I promise that I won't touch a hair on your head, Freddie." I held the pack through the fence. "I just want to talk a while."

For the next fifteen minutes I sweated, hoping I'd be able to swap a cigarette or two for at least a few more moments of his life. A human life is such a valuable and precious commodity, more valuable than all the riches of the world, more valuable than gold or diamonds, more valuable than all the money in the world stacked in one huge pile. It's so valuable, in fact, that a God left heaven, became a man, and died on a cross to give Freddie, me, and all of us life—real life.

"O.K.," Freddie said at last. "Come on over the fence; but that's all—ya hear?"

The fence had an entrance door about fifteen yards away, but there was a big, rusty padlock and chain on it. I looked over to the hotel manager, and he responded with a helpless gesture that told me, "We don't have the key!"

Pulling a nearby wooden bench close to the fence, I hauled myself up, got a leg over the top of the jagged links, and to the tune of ripping cloth, dropped down six feet to the other side. I walked over to the ledge where Freddie was sitting and stopped about three feet away from him. He looked even younger than he had from a distance. He also looked damned determined. I held out the pack of cigarettes and he took one.

And then he began to smoke—and talk. And smoke and talk.

Over the past ten years I have read and studied just about everything that the "experts" have had to say about suicides—motivation and prevention. Some of the nonsense I've seen has been so textbookish and farfetched that I find myself wondering if any of those so-called pros have ever personally dealt with a real, honest-to-God suicide threat. I wonder if they ever sat face to face with a man or woman who really wanted to—and was about to—destroy himself. The "experts" make up lists of all possible reasons *why* the person would be in a suicide position in the first place; but they don't offer too many good recipes for getting him out of, or down from, a place of immediate peril.

I wonder how many of those experts, psychologists, psychiatrists, or social workers have any kind of grasp of man's second, but very real, life: his spiritual life. Call it his soul or spirit or psyche if you like—that part of man, created directly by God, which is like Himself; that part of man that will never die, no matter how many floors a man might plunge. The thought of eternity is a *forever* that is mighty real.

And I always wind up wondering if the experts discount the real presence of the Holy Spirit at the suicide scene— He who gives the grace, who inspires the right words. He, who, as St. Paul reminds us, "breathes and moves where He will—"

It began to get chilly up there on the roof. The crowds were larger now, and I could see people hanging out of office building windows, some with binoculars, hesitant to leave for home, fearful that they might miss a juicy slice of human drama. The roof of a hotel was the stage; the blue sky was the proscenium arch; neighboring skyscrapers were the backdrop. It might have been twenty minutes, it might have been an hour that we talked, listened, prayed, and reasoned with this disturbed young man.

I finally said, "Jeez, Fred, I'm getting cold. I'm going to see if there's some hot coffee back there. Want some?"

"No."

"O.K. Wait here for me, willya?"

A policeman from the emergency unit and the worried hotel manager met me at the fence, and I told them what I needed. In minutes they were back with two cups of steaming hot black coffee.

"What do you think, Father?" the cop from the crash truck whispered.

I shook my head. "I really can't figure him. One moment, I'm sure he's going. The next, he's talking about riding the Wild Mouse at the beach with his wife."

"We found the wife, Lucy. She thinks he's putting on an act. She'll talk to him—but not up here."

"Some act. If the wind changes, he's gone. And I promised him that I wouldn't touch a hair on his head!"

And as I turned to carry the coffee back toward the distraught youth, the cop warned me, "Watch yourself, ya hear?"

Yeah, I heard, but I also heard Christ's words scrambling around in the back of my head, "Whoever lays down his life for his friends . . ."

The sun was dipping fast, and I felt that something was going to happen, probably very quickly. Every time I threw a lifeline out to him, out to this kid drowning in his own sea of screwed-up emotions, fears, loneliness, and frustrations, he had carefully, deliberately cut it.

All of a sudden, he began to cry. Quietly, tears began to run down his cheeks and splashed somewhere between the eighteenth and first floors. "God—I ain't no good; I ain't nothin'." And then, just as suddenly, he grew furious and began to curse and swear. He began sending people to hell: the whole world; his mother-in-law; his wife; himself—and the chaplain.

I held out another cigarette.

"Light it for me," he snapped.

Standing three feet away from him as he held the now-cold cup of coffee in one hand, I lit a Winston and handed it to him. He took the cigarette and looked me in the eye. "I really want to thank you for coming up here and listening to me. Let me ask you somethin'. Can people in hell pray for people back here in this life?"

I saw a new, strange look come into his eyes. I watched him very closely. My heart pounded faster. Adrenaline started to flow. Something told me that the drama was about to peak—fast.

I was saying, "Let's you and me go down to the rectory, and we'll meet Lucy there. I promise I—"

But Freddie wasn't listening. At least not to me.

Perhaps it was that supersecond before one acts on impulse: an eerie light seemed to illumine his face, a half-smile curled his lips, and with wide, wild eyes, he raised his head and looked up—and his body swayed forward.

That's when I moved.

I hit him from the side with every bit of strength I had.

My right shoulder crashed into his right side. A terrible yell escaped from his lips when he realized what happened, and it seemed that he tried to bring us both over that precipice. For a sickening, awful moment, I thought that I had misjudged and that the force of the tackle would carry us both over the edge. For a terrible, agonizing second, we teetered on the top of that eight-inch ledge. He struggled, but both my arms were around him in a viselike grip, and I wasn't about to let go. After what seemed forever, I threw him over to the roofside, with two hundred pounds of tattered black suit pinning him down.

As he struggled, cried, and cursed, I heard the police scrambling over the fence and footsteps racing across the roof to assist us. One of the cops put his knee on Fred's throat and twisted his arm behind his back—way up behind his back.

I panted, "Hey—easy, fellows. He's not going anywhere. Take it easy!"

We carried him, kicking and screaming, to a small room near the elevators, and he looked at me through glazed and anguished eyes.

"You—you lied to me! I trusted you. You said that you wouldn't touch me. You lied to me!"

I'll never forget that look. As I wiped his grimy face and tears with my handkerchief, I gasped, "No, Freddie; I said that I wouldn't touch a hair on your head—and I didn't. I knew you weren't listening to me out there. I had to—to—get your attention."

The police radioed in a Code 4 on the scene and began the business of getting his name, address, age, driver's license, etc. I listened to all this for a few minutes; then I asked the sergeant to step over in the corner.

"There are no charges here, are there?" I asked.

"I dunno, Padre. I thought I'd book him and hold him for a coroner's examination. Besides, he created a pretty good 103 [disturbing the peace] and one helluva 23 [traffic jam] downstairs."

"For God's sake, Mike!" I exploded. "This man is sick, and there are all kinds of sicknesses. Forget the charges and let him come with me. I guarantee I'll be responsible."

"I dunno, Padre. The regs—"

"Get your rank on the phone and let me talk to him, O.K.?"

I went back to Fred as the sergeant went to the phone.

"They're gonna bust me, aren't they? Thanks a lot—that's all I need now!" And he turned his head away.

There was a long, bitter silence till the sergeant returned.

"O.K., Father, he's all yours. Captain Farrell wants you to call him later, though."

"Appreciate it, Mike—whenever you're ready, we'll go Fred. There's no problem now."

"Jeez—" was all that the man could utter.

As I was brushing off my suit, Daley from the emergency unit came up and said, "Hell, I haven't seen a tackle like that since I played at old Saint Aloysius'."

"Priest power, Richard!" I said, grinning.

For the first time that afternoon, Freddie half-smiled as he tried to hold another hot cup of coffee in his trembling hands. "I remember back in grammar school," he recalled, "a nun once told us the story of the guy that was knocked off his horse on his ass. And then he had a whole new life."

"Right, Freddie. And that guy's name was Paul—Saint Paul."

But I didn't feel good. As I led Fred to the elevators and a meeting with him and Lucy and later with a psychiatrist at the rectory, a haunting thought, an accusing thought that was to keep me awake for many nights, flashed through my mind: *Did* I lie to this man? Or was it the only way out?"

Was it?

CHAPTER 14

Trilogy of Tragedy

TRAGEDY OFTEN DOES NOT WALK ALONE. In this fabulous, fast, and charming city of New Orleans, a city which I have grown to love very deeply, there have been multiple tragedies, tragic happenings in which not one person met violent death or injury—but many.

Three of these stand out vividly:

11:00 P.M.

The TV late movie that night was *The Pink Submarine* and Fr. Don Haile and I, half-asleep, were watching it in the community room, when Headquarters phoned on Line 2.

"Father—they request you on a Code 2 over in the Quarter. All hell has broke loose. Somebody has driven up Bourbon Street—reports say that at least ten people are down!"

I ran to the police radio in my office and finally got in on Channel 1.

"Car 30, as best we can determine, the last victim is on Bourbon and Toulouse streets. The vehicle crashed there, and the occupants ran. Would suggest you go to Toulouse and work your way down to Canal."

"Car 30 here. That's 10-04—what happened?"

"Not sure yet; all we know is someone drove up Bourbon at a high rate of speed."

"God—Bourbon Street is a pedestrian mall at night."

"That's 10-04, Car 30!"

In a matter of minutes, I was heading up Toulouse toward Bourbon—five blocks away. I parked with two wheels up on the sidewalk, and Officer Joe Hurban, on his three-wheeler motorcycle, pulled up beside me. He told me that two teenagers—about sixteen or seventeen years old—had stolen an automobile up on Washington Avenue, and Car 216 had spotted them and given chase.

"Car 216 followed them all over town—the kids wouldn't stop. It's a miracle no one was killed. All of a sudden they turned off Canal into Bourbon—went right through the barricades. You can see what happened!"

"Pull your bike out in the middle of the street, will you please, Joe?"

I jumped up on the back of his three-wheeler and from that vantage point, looked down Bourbon Street toward Canal.

I couldn't believe my eyes. Lying on the ground—down the six-block area—were about twelve or fifteen persons, every fifty or hundred yards. Each victim was surrounded by a group of people—friends or passersby—trying to render aid. It looked like a dozen suffering, agonizing huddles.

I opened the sick call set and placed the purple stole around my neck. Sitting behind Joe on the rear of his motorcycle, stole fluttering like the Lord's banner, and clutching the sick call set, we began our ride. Joe sped me to each of the persons who had been struck and hurled to the pavement by the speeding car.

The victims were in shock, disbelief, and pain. Some were seriously hurt; others merely had suffered glancing blows as they'd tried to scramble out of the path of the careening auto.

Out for a night stroll on the famous Rue Bourbon, these victims were now suddenly faced with pain, suffering, and possibly, death. For those who were conscious, I asked each if he or she would like me to pray *with* him and *for* him. No one refused.

I gave all the injured persons absolution, after asking them to be sorry for any serious sins they might have committed against their God. And placing on their foreheads the holy oils and saying the Prayer of the Sick, I gave them the special blessing for the sick and suffering. As I ministered to each victim, I noticed a young woman moving from victim to victim, efficiently and gently doing a good job of making each as comfortable as possible.

If the victim had a friend or family member with them, I told them who I was, tried to comfort *them,* got their name and address, and told them that I would see them later at Charity Hospital. And Joe and I cycled off again to the next victim.

Ambulances and emergency units began arriving from Charity and Family Health, besides our own police and fire units. They darted about, treating each victim, and placed them in their units.

I stopped the fire unit. "Fellows, I've seen them all. I think the fifth one down—white male, about twenty-five— is in real bad shape. Maybe you should check him first."

Later, in Charity's emergency room, despite every effort by the doctors, that victim of the mad ride expired. I phoned his family in Memphis and softly broke the sad news to them. Sorrowfully, unbelievingly, they said that they would be here in the morning.

Two hours later, as I was leaving the hospital, I spotted the young woman whom I had seen at the scene treating the victims. She told me that she was a nurse from Chicago, and I commended her on the fine job she had done in making so many of the victims comfortable, taking pulses and keeping an eye on them until the units took them to the hospital.

"Never again. Never again will I try to be nice."

I asked her why.

"You know why?" She smiled, but it was a bitter smile.

"As I was treating one of the victims, I laid my purse, with all my money and credit cards, to the side. When I finished my work, I found that someone had stolen it!"

1:00 A.M.

The huge Delta DC8 had arrived from Chicago at 11:34 P.M. at New Orleans' International Airport, and 105 people and crew poured out. It had been a pleasant and relaxing flight for the passengers; but now five pilots had to take the plane aloft again with a Federal Aviation Inspector for a routine inspection flight. But it was not routine—not for the six men who were aboard, nor for nine high school kids and three other guests of the Hilton Inn.

On the last turn, preparing to land, the huge airship suddenly swerved down. With a thunderous roar, the plane hit the ground about one mile from the runway. It demolished the homes of Truman Shaggs and Shelley Whittington, plus a garage, before it careened wildly, sickeningly, across an open field and into the Hilton Inn.

The high schoolers, from Juda, Wisconsin, were on their senior class trip. Earlier in the year they had unanimously voted that enchanting New Orleans was the place they would like to visit. Full of life and eager for excitement, they arrived in the Crescent City on the morning of March 30.

The youngsters were keenly disappointed, however, when they found out that the motel in which they held reservations did not have a swimming pool. They asked their chaperones and counselors if another hotel could be found—one where they could swim and enjoy even more the balmy New Orleans days and nights.

After some hurried phone calls, they were told that the Hilton Inn at the airport could accommodate the thirty-two high-schoolers and their adult supervisors. Gleefully the kids checked into their new abode—and headed for the swimming pool.

That evening, some decided to tour downtown New Orleans, but many preferred to stay and splash in the luxurious pool. They admired the gorgeous Louisiana sunset as darkness fell, but for nine of the Wisconsin students, there would never be another sunrise.

The crippled airliner hit with a terrible explosion and seconds later came crashing into the rear of the Hilton, into the section where the Wisconsin kids had been lodged.

"It was awful! We didn't know what happened. Then there was fire every place."

The screaming of terrified people mingled with the moans of the dying.

Shock and disbelief paralyzed other hotel guests and waitresses, bellmen, and desk clerks. The switchboard operators and kitchen employees in the unscathed front part of the hotel then began phoning and knocking on the doors of the rooms in the rear section.

A First District car sped me to the airport disaster.

"Father, you'll never get through the traffic jam by yourself," Headquarters had phoned. "We'll send Car 103 to get you out there."

I called a number of ministers and priests who had churches near the airport and asked them also to come to the scene of the tragedy.

A state policeman told me that there were some bodies in the field behind the motel—these were the Delta crew and the inspector. Firemen from Jefferson Parish, the airport, Kenner, and New Orleans were all there.

At one point in our search, a fireman's flashlight pinpointed still another grim discovery: the right hand of one of the victims. Only the hand.

After attending as many victims as could be found, I

joined a group of rescuers who were searching the rooms of the Hilton immediately after the fires had been put out. The acrid, sickening smell of burned flesh was everywhere.

A Jefferson deputy took me to one of the rooms. "Take a look in here, Chaplain," he said.

There were three or four young and charred bodies, huddled together in the shower. They held each other close in a last, desperate effort to stay alive in the blazing fires and explosions that followed the crash. A trickle of water from the shower dripped on their bodies—a last, silent ablution to their youth and to their togetherness—together even in death.

In many cases the only things that served as IDs were their new senior rings, which they all proudly wore. Inside the gold band the kids had their names or initials engraved.

I spent the rest of the night with the survivors, helping to phone anguished parents and relatives, when finally we were able to ascertain positive identification.

The people of Juda, that peaceful and quiet Wisconsin town, were in shock and in mourning for a long, long time. The entire population attended the nine funerals for the youths—those beautiful, young American kids who loved to swim.

10:47 A.M.

The shootings occurred on the last day of the autumn Solemn Novena. It was November 7, 1977, or to put it another way, as a gambler might: 7-11—except in this instance, the fateful numbers didn't prove lucky.

Between the morning and the noon services of the Solemn Novena there is a two-hour break, and I ducked out to Joe the barber to get a haircut. As I returned to the rectory, with the police radio on, I heard a motorcycle policeman shout, "There's a 34-S on Bourbon Street; the 200 block. There are three or four people down. Get some units over here right away—on a Code 3."

I wheeled the Ford, blue lights flashing and siren yelping, over to Bourbon and pulled in before the emergency units arrived. I noticed that a green Oldsmobile was parked in the middle of Bourbon Street, the driver nowhere to be seen.

"Father—over here!" yelled Patrolman Roy Guggenheim of the three-wheelers.

I saw three men lying on the ground in Edison Plaza, a small parklike area on busy Bourbon Street. One was an elderly tourist from Alabama. His wife knelt by his side, holding his hand. The other two victims of this mysterious shooting were friends from Nashville, Tennessee, visiting New Orleans for the first time.

Two of the three were conscious, but in extreme pain. I prayed and tried to soothe each one; gave them all absolution, the Sacrament of the Sick, and the Last Blessing. When the units arrived, I helped carry the victims to the ambulances.

Seeing the elderly man's wife standing dazed and alone on the sidewalk, I asked her, "Would you like to ride with him to Charity Hospital? I'll meet you there in a little while."

"Yes, sir," she automatically said, and I helped her into the unit beside her bleeding man. "Why did that stranger shoot my husband? My husband never hurt a soul. We were planning to go back to Alabama tomorrow."

After the two younger victims were also whisked to Charity, I watched and listened as the detectives checked out the Olds that had been abandoned in the middle of the street and talked to witnesses. They soon received some further information on radio from Headquarters.

"That's it. He's the guy, apparently," said Detective Eugene Fields.

"What's it all about?" I asked.

"About two hours ago a man, separated from his wife, went to her father's home uptown—on Adams Street. He allegedly shot his father-in-law and then pumped three shots into his wife, Diana, who was sleeping in bed."

"They dead?"

"No, but both are in real bad shape at Charity. This here is his car. Apparently after he shot them, he flipped; got into his car, came down here to Bourbon Street, and shot three total strangers!"

"Where is he now?" a reporter from WWL-TV asked.

"He ran up Bourbon Street. We've got everyone alerted. God knows who, or if, or when, he might hit again."

The human mind is a delicate and complicated piece of machinery given to us by God. Severe tension or stress or sorrow or frustration are some of the pressures that can trigger a malfunction. It is a difficult thing to know when a person is acting logically, sanely, and in total possession and control of his mind, and the split second when something snaps, and the thinking and reasoning process is disrupted or deranged.

When the man shot the three strangers on Bourbon Street, he ran toward Rampart Street. Near the Lafitte Housing Project, he stole an automobile belonging to a Clem Weston and headed back into the central business district. He parked the stolen car in a nearby lot and, again for some strange, mysterious reason, walked into the investment offices of the Charles Darwin Fenner Management Corporation on Common Street.

Without a word to anyone, he pulled the shiny .38 automatic from his belt and fired. He first hit an employee of the investment company, and then at close range, pumped two shots into a customer who was sitting at a desk. The seventy-six-year-old man quietly slumped to the floor. The gunman then calmly walked to an adjacent desk and fired point-blank at another investment consultant.

The gunman then sprinted to the door, as a roomful of horrified people looked on in stunned silence. Out on Common Street, which was crowded with the noontime rush, he next turned the weapon on Robert Barrell, Douglas Martin, and then Hans Anderson of Norway. Witnesses on the crowded street said that it appeared that one of them had attempted to stop the running gunman, and all were shot down at close range.

I was just returning to St. Jude's from the shootings on Bourbon Street to help with the twelve o'clock novena service, when I picked up the report of these later shootings. I headed for Common Street.

Four minutes later, Car 30 was parked on Canal Street's neutral ground, and I sprinted the remaining block to Common Street, black sick call kit under my arm.

Police helped me through the large crowds that were standing in shocked disbelief, wondering, guessing what it was all about. After giving the last rites to the men on the sidewalk and speaking to the two victims who were conscious, I helped the ambulance attendants as they ministered to the victims—gently holding the heads of some as the medics wrapped the wounds to prevent more loss of blood. We then carried the stretchers to the waiting units.

The customer inside the brokerage house looked extremely bad. The police unit sped him to Charity as quickly as possible. I later got his home address from the firm's business office, phoned his elderly sister, and visited him again later at Charity. Two days later, he died.

As I bent low over another victim, something about him looked vaguely familiar. He was shot in the eye, and the bullet had emerged behind his ear. His ashen face was covered with blood. I whispered the words of contrition and gave him conditional absolution, assuring him that he would make it and to "hang in there." He could not speak, but his eyes said "Thanks."

I later saw him at Baptist Hospital, and when he had regained consciousness, chatted with him. *I* chatted; his mouth was tightly wired, and there was a mountain of gauze around his head.

"When I saw you out there, I knew there was something familiar about you," I told him. He reached for a pencil and laboriously wrote, "You married Terri Ann and me five years ago at St. Jude's!"

Meanwhile, the gunman, after emptying his gun at the last victim on the sidewalk, ran wildly across Common Street toward the Sears store. Two vice squad policemen, Bill Schultz and Stanford Barre, in plainclothes and unmarked car, were cruising nearby when the report of the shootings came in. They drove over near Common and Baronne and as they stopped their car, saw a man running toward them, trying to stuff a revolver in his belt.

"Police—freeze!" they shouted.

The gunman seemed bewildered; he looked around as if they were talking to someone else. Then he slowly put his hands up.

"It's a good thing he didn't go for his weapon," Schultz later said. "If he did, he was dead!"

The sad, mystifying total of this unexplainable tragedy: eleven shot—one soon to die and two probably paralyzed for life. Of the eleven persons shot that morning, the gunman had never seen nine of them in his life.

Tragedy often does not walk alone. But in the unpredictable yet lovable city of New Orleans, when tragedy does walk the streets, Car 30 is there to try to bring some of Christ's peace and love and reason to some unreasonable and unexplainable acts of violence.

CHAPTER 15

The Horn on the '41 Ford

7:23 *P.M.*

DET. JOSEPH ROBERT TARDIFF, JR., age twenty-seven, should not have been killed that night on St. Peter's Street in the French Quarter. He was killed because he was too dedicated, too fearless, too much cop.

Five weeks earlier Joe and his partner had answered a 107 call—suspicious persons—in the Magnolia Housing Project. They found a burglary in progress, and a shoot-out followed. Tardiff was shot in the stomach, but as he fell, he pumped three shots at the fleeing thugs. One of the assailants dropped: dead.

Joe spent one week in serious condition at Charity Hospital; later he was sent home to mend further for three more weeks. He was anxious to return to duty, but he was given an office job at Headquarters. His captain wanted him to have more time to recuperate before being sent back on the street.

Two weeks after returning to work at Headquarters, Tardiff picked up a call of a possible 64-G, an armed robbery, at Dominick's Shell Station, across the street from the church of Our Lady of Guadalupe. I bumped into Joe, whom I had visited four weeks earlier in Charity Hospital, by the gas pumps at Dominick's.

"I didn't know you were back on the street, Joe," I said.

"Shhh—it's a big secret, Padre," he grinned. "I can't stay away from the action. Filing stolen bicycle reports in an office at Headquarters is my idea of nothing."

Shots sounded beyond a wall behind Dominick's, and a

detective shouted, "He's back here; he's armed and is firing at us!"

The wall was at least ten-feet high, and on top of it, imbedded in cement, were broken, jagged pieces of glass to discourage intruders.

"Let's go, Padre," Joe urged. "Boost me up."

I hesitated. I knew that there was a gaping hole in the man's stomach, not completely healed, covered only with gauze and tape. A fence-climbing caper could possibly rip open the wound.

"Joe, don't be nuts. Let the other guys—"

"Please, Padre—he's over there!"

Reluctantly I went to the wall and clasped my hands, stirruplike, in front of me. In a matter of minutes Joe was up and over. But not before ripping his arm on one of the pieces of jagged glass that was imbedded on top of the wall.

One hour later they found the trapped suspect in a tiny room on the ground floor of a nearby house where he was hiding.

Tardiff dropped by the rectory later that night, a bandage on his right arm, and softly said, "Don't mention this to Jewel. She and the kids might not understand."

Jewel was his wife, very much in love with her husband and devoted to their three children, Julianne, eleven; Tracy, eight; and little Troy, four. They had recently bought a new home in New Orleans East, and life seemed so rosy—everything was going so good! But Jewel worried about her cop-husband. He loved his home, loved her, loved the children, loved to fool with antique cars. He was happy. But yet she worried at times.

While he was at work, she would look out the window at the vintage car, a 1941 Ford coupe, that Joe was working on. He had renewed it, painted it, polished it, caressed it, driven it up and down the streets. He had everything in perfect condition, except one thing: He was looking for a special horn. A horn that would make a very special sound—for that very special car.

But still Jewel worried. Like many policemen's wives, she wondered, "Does he love his police work more than us?" Even when he was off duty, he lived and breathed police business. He was total cop.

On the night of February 28, 1975, Julianne was in a talent show at her school, St. James Major. Joe had dropped by to visit his mother, and Jewel had driven over to her parents' house. Her father was a retired firefighter, Warren Luc. While she was there, she phoned Joe at his mother's.

"I'm going down to Headquarters," he told her. "I have to fill out some papers on that humbug at Dominick's Service Station a couple of nights ago. Be back soon."

"O.K., darling. I told the children that we'd take them for a ride later. Thought we might go over to Lake Forest Plaza and watch the people ice-skate."

"Sounds good, honey. Then we'll get some ice cream. See ya later—and hey, I love you!"

I received the call on the police radio as a 95-G. A man— possibly a sniper—was in the 600 block of Rampart Street, firing a gun. Leaving Car 30 in the carport, I walked down the three blocks. Police were everywhere.

It later was shown that the gunman, Darrell Doiron, had been arrested and convicted four times recently. On that wild night in the Quarter, he shot and killed an innocent woman, Patti Hoffman, as she walked with her husband to the Theatre of the Performing Arts.

Doiron also shot and wounded two detectives, John Kastner and Pete Mankiewicz, when they stopped to question him about some previous robberies.

"He's on top of that apartment house on Rampart," one policeman said.

"He just ran around the block. I think he's on top of the Maison Dupuy Hotel," another man stated.

"He's back on Burgundy Street—the 700 block," still another insisted.

They soon found out where the gunman *was* hiding—and where he was about to die. Darrell Doiron had just broken into a second-story apartment in the 1000 block of St. Peter's Street. It was to be his last address on this earth.

Chief Clarence Giarrusso was personally directing the attack. I stood by him on that charming French Quarter street. Powerful spotlights were trained on the apartment, as Giarrusso listened to the various reports coming in. He talked on a bullhorn to the ambushed gunman, pleading with him to surrender, to come out with his hands up.

Another volley of shots was heard, and the report soon came in that an officer who was trying to reach the upstairs apartment by the outside stairway had been hit.

They were able to get to Joe Tardiff about a half-hour later. I was with him as they frantically put his limp body into the waiting crash truck.

"Is he dead, Father?" someone asked.

"No, he's still breathing. I think."

"Where the hell is the driver of this goddamned unit?" screamed one of Tardiff's buddies.

"He went around to the back to look for him," someone shouted.

"Who is it?" asked Chief Turner.

"Tardiff. Joe Tardiff."

"My God, he's supposed to be off duty!" Turner said.

A young detective, I think it was Robert McNeill, jumped in the driver's seat. "Never drove one of these, but here goes. Hang on, Padre!"

As I knelt beside the bleeding and dying officer, we took off—no, we *flew* off—for Charity Hospital. Crossing busy Canal Street, we were almost hit broadside by a speeding taxi that screechingly stopped just inches from us. Mc-Neill's responses to the cabby were not at all in the same key as my prayers for the dying man.

I held Joe in my arms so that he wouldn't fall off the stretcher, and I whispered in his ear, "Jesus, Mary, and Joseph. My Lord, I love You. Jesus, forgive me all my sins. I am sorry. I am sorry. Forgive me." And I pronounced those words which give hope and comfort and reconciliation: "And by His authority, I forgive you all your sins, in the name of the Father and of the Son and of the Holy Spirit."

Det. Joe Tardiff died as he was being wheeled into the emergency room.

I waited till the doctors officially pronounced him dead, and then I hitched a police ride back to the scene, where I told Chief Giarrusso. He bowed his head and closed his eyes.

"Joe Tardiff didn't even have to be here tonight. He was off duty."

A sergeant ran up. "Chief, the gunman, a guy named Doiron, is dead. The body's up in the kitchen."

The chief turned to me. "Padre, you might want to give him the last rites, too. Or something."

"I'll go up there now. Then I've got to tell Jewel, Joe's wife, before she sees it on the news."

"I'll go with you when you're ready," the chief said.

Jewel had picked up her daughter Julianne after the dance rehearsal and headed home. She claims now that she had had a "funny feeling" but couldn't quite explain it. As she pulled in beside the old Ford in the driveway, she saw her policeman neighbor, Allen Latapie, pacing up and down outside. He was listening to his police radio.

"Anything wrong, Allen?" she asked fearfully.

"There's been some humbug downtown. Don't know much about it yet," he said evasively.

She put the kids in the car and drove to nearby Methodist Hospital. If his stomach wound had opened, he might have gone there. But his car was nowhere to be seen.

For some unknown reason, she recalls, she grasped her three little people around her. "Children, I don't know why, but I have a feeling that something has happened to Daddy. Let's say a little prayer."

Of all the tasks that are asked of the police and fire chaplain, none is more heavy—none is more sad—than breaking the news to a woman that her man has been killed. There is no "way" to break the sad news. There is no formula, no written script. Each one is different. And each one becomes more difficult.

As we drove out I-10 to Jewel Tardiff's home the names of some of the police and fire widows that I have been with in their bitter sorrow over the years paraded through my mind in silent formation: Stone, Puderer, Aymami, Forstall, McInerney, Coleman, Persigo, Sirgo, Archer, Pellegrin, Bergeron, Zinger, Harrell, Pinero, Poirier, Boudreaux, Vernolt, Brady, Hosli, Polito, Verret, Belsom . . . These names are not only emblazoned on the honor rolls which hang in Our Lady of Guadalupe Church, but each is remembered daily at the Eucharist by their chaplain in behalf of a community which should be eternally grateful.

When I pulled Car 30 to a stop in front of the Tardiff home, it was a little after 10:00 P.M. Four-year-old Troy was playing outside on the front lawn. It was a quiet, balmy Louisiana night, and the little boy was certainly not ready for bed. He ran toward the chief and me and took my hand.

"Com'ere," he said. "I want to show you something!" And he led us over to the carport where the old Ford silently stood. "My daddy fixed it all up," he declared. "And you know what? Look what he put on yesterday."

He jumped into the driver's seat and sounded the new horn that Joe Tardiff had installed: a horn that he would never again hear.

The boy squealed in sheer delight when the *ah-hoo-gaa* blasted.

We rang the front doorbell, and Julianne opened the door. "Yes?" she asked shyly.

"Is your mother home, honey?" I asked.

Jewel came out of the kitchen holding a towel. She looked at the chief, then at me. A loud shriek came from her lips. Then she bolted and ran through the dining area, down a corridor, and into the bedroom where she locked the door.

A few of the neighbors came in and gathered the three children into their arms, while I gently told them that their daddy had gone to heaven just a little while ago.

Mrs. Latapie, the next-door neighbor who was married to a policeman, brushed back her tears and went to make some coffee. I headed for the locked-in, grieving wife.

She was crying and sobbing and screaming.

I put my mouth close to the door. "Jewel, please come out. I want to tell you something." I continued to talk softly; I tried to soothe, to search for the right words of comfort.

After about ten minutes, she unlocked the door. "I'm—I'm sorry," she said, holding a damp cloth to her eyes. "Tell me about it. I had a funny feeling ever since I talked to him earlier tonight."

I put my arm around her shoulders and led her back to the living room where we sat down. Mrs. Latapie poured some coffee.

The chief quietly described what had happened. All the while that he was speaking, Jewel was slowly shaking her head from side to side, as if to say, "That's him; that's how he would act."

Giarrusso concluded, "And I know it won't change anything, but the other officers told me how your husband pushed one detective out of the line of fire—then was hit himself."

Jewel looked at me as she hugged little Troy to her breast. "What am I going to do, Father? I don't think I can make it without him." And tears silently ran down her face.

"Yes, you'll make it, Jewel. You've got to make it—for your own sake, for their sakes, and for him." And I looked directly in her eyes and said, "And don't ever sell that old car. The one with the horn."

Jewel tried to smile. "I promise you—and him. I never will!"

Today, Jewel Tardiff and her three children proudly drive that '41 Ford in the antique auto parades and vintage car events. And Troy, now eight, still likes to blast the funny horn.

But he doesn't do it too often.

Because everytime he does, his mommy cries.

CHAPTER 16

Quartet in a Washroom

5:32 P.M.

It was during the Saturday Vigil Mass, just after Communion, that lovely, quiet time when man communes with his Savior, trying to say "thank you" for the world's most beautiful gift.

Deacon Melvin Jones approached the altar where I was standing and put a note down near the chalice. "Emergency — Hostage Situation — Maison Blanche."

In New Orleans as well as in many other cities, the police chaplain is an ex officio member of the S.W.A.T. (Special Weapons And Tactics) team, a specially trained and equipped group of police officers. They are present at shoot-outs, Superbowl games, Mardi Gras parades, kidnappings, and hostage-takings. They are trained to scale buildings with a single line, and they use special arms ranging from a tiny pistol in their socks to the explosive M-16. Their uniform is a dark fatigue suit and a baseball cap with the letters S.T. on the front. They are the city's top cops.

Immediately after Mass, only a few moments more, I headed for the department store, which had been located at the corner of Canal and Dauphine for over seventy years. The S.W.A.T. team had surrounded the building already. It was after closing time, and they urged the puzzled pedestrians to move on.

Calvin Galliano, the youthful but experienced captain of the S.W.A.T. team, met me at the escalator.

"Seems that a young white male entered the women's rest room right before closing time," said Cal, briefing me as we rose to the second floor. "He chased all the women out — except one. He's got her in there now."

The biggest question mark in a hostage situation is that the police don't know who they are up against. Is the perpetrator high on drugs or booze? Is he someone trying to get a message to the world via the media? Is he a frustrated lover trying to accept a rejection? Is he merely putting on a show to impress a wife or girl friend? Is he a psychopathic killer, a madman unable to control impulse, mind, and action?

In such a situation a game plan is worked out. Established patterns are put into action. Perimeters are set up. The command post is centrally located. Troops are deployed strategically. And the negotiator gets the starring role.

"Paul Melancon's in the john now. He's the negotiator."

The negotiator must have a cool head. He must be glib yet believable, smooth-talking yet sincere. He musn't make promises he can't keep. He must never forget that the man he is talking to might have a knife or a gun or explosives at the head of a terrified hostage. The wrong word could mean death.

As I moved through the crowd of S.W.A.T. people outside the rest room, I saw Dan Lincove, the manager of Maison Blanche, walking nervously, hands clasped behind his back, near a counter where sandals were on sale.

"The guy says to let the priest in," Officer John Marie told Galliano. "He'll talk to him."

Sometimes but not always, the police chaplain has a definite role as negotiator. This and a lot of other things I learned when I attended not long before an F.B.I. seminar in Quantico, Virginia. Skilled and experienced agents gave a course on hostage negotiations to twenty-five police chaplains from around the country. When a chaplain does become a negotiator, it's not time for a pious sermonette or "dear brother, why are you doing this?" It's a time for action, and the chaplain better have the right words.

"Go on in, Padre," said Galliano, "but watch yourself."

I walked through the door marked "women" and entered a private little world, standing in the center of which was a man with blond hair, about twenty-five or so.

"Hi," I said, trying to sound as casual as I could. Seated on a chair in front of him was an attractive young girl. He had his left arm around her neck, and he held in his right hand a long-bladed knife against her jugular vein. Her eyes met mine, and the message she flashed was HELP ME.

"Hi, Paul," I said to the officer, who was standing about four feet in front of them.

"Where ya at, Father?"

"That's far enough, preacher," the young man snapped.

I stopped right where I was and asked what was going on. The young man told us he just got into town from Denver. The woman he was living with had thrown him out and told him he could return when he had money enough to take care of her and her two kids.

"My name is Fr. Rogers. What's yours?"

"David Gray," said the young man with an ice-cold stare.

"Hey," said Melancon, "you just told me it was Robert Triggs."

I began to talk about Denver and what a beautiful place Colorado was and the Oblates had a parish in the Springs about forty-five minutes south of Denver.

"What is this, a goddamn travelogue? I brought you in here for one reason, preacher. Get the money — or this chick is dead."

"Look, David," said Melancon, leaning casually against one of the toilet stalls, "we've been talking for half an hour, and I'm really beginning to like you." He flashed a smile that would have disarmed the Ayatollah Khomeini.

Trying to use as best we could the finest weapon a negotiator has, time, we talked and talked. David or Robert made his demands again and again. He wanted $20,000 in small bills, a car filled with gas parked in front of the store, and if no one followed him, he would release the girl somewhere outside of town. He seemed mystified that we had trouble understanding them.

Half an hour passed. He was getting jittery. Blood began to trickle down the girl's throat where the knife had nicked her skin. I was getting worried. But Melancon, if he was bothered, didn't show it. If anything, he seemed more casual and detached than before.

"Look," said Melancon, "I'm going out to see if the store has that kind of money lying around. All the banks are closed by now. It's Saturday, you know."

"Don't bullshit me, man! Saturday is a busy day in any department store. They have the money here. Now move!"

Melancon left, and I began to talk to the young girl — Kathy was her name — and found out that she had recently been graduated from the University of New Orleans and was looking for a job. She lived with her parents. Resurrection of the Lord parish. The more we chatted, the more she calmed down. David, however, was getting more agitated.

"You've got twenty minutes!" he shouted.

"David, would you like me to get you something?" I looked at his arms and did not see any needle tracks, but I didn't want to overlook anything that might help resolve the situation. "Some pills, T's and Blues, a stick, anything? It might help you now."

"Preacher, the only thing I want is the money and to get out of this f------ town. Go see what's holding that cop up."

"He'll be right back." I didn't want to leave him alone with the girl. "Paul's a good man, and he'll be right back."

Outside, Melancon was filling in the police brass and the Maison Blanche officials.

"Let's give him the money and get him out of the store."

"He's not going to leave this store with the girl, and that's for sure."

"We may have a chance for a shot at him."

"Why blast him away?" asked Melancon. "He hasn't hurt anybody. Besides, the girl's sitting directly in front of him."

Everyone seemed to have a different answer.

The girl's parents had arrived. They were sitting not too far away from the rest room door.

"Hello," said Melancon walking over to them. "Kathy's fine, and she said to tell you hi." Their faces were chalky with fear and a helpless sort of dread. "Fr. Rogers, our chaplain, is in there with them now."

"Is she safe?" asked her mother, an attractive woman in her mid-forties. She held a rosary in her hand.

"She's a real trooper. Please try not to worry too much. We're doing the very best we can." Melancon chatted with them for a few minutes. Together they said three Hail Marys. Then he left them and rejoined the quarterbacks planning the next play.

"Did they get the money?" asked Melancon.

"Mr. Lincove is bringing it up," said Galliano. "It shouldn't be too much longer."

It was eight o'clock before Melancon reentered the rest room. Kathy was crying softly. I was still chattering on. David was angry, about to explode.

"The money's on its way, David. In the meantime, why not let me walk you to the car. Leave the girl here. She'd only be in your way."

David laughed, then cursed.

Fifteen more minutes passed before a shopping bag emblazoned with "I've shopped and saved at Maison Blanche" was dropped inside the rest room door.

"I don't know if it's all here," said Melancon, "but I think we ought to count it."

How long does it take to count twenty thousand dollars in small bills, I wondered. I was edgy, but I was taking all my cues from Melancon.

"The hell you'll count it!"

"Well, what'll I do with it?"

"Dump it in her lap, that's what," he exploded. "Is the car down there?"

"Yeah, they said it's at the door."

Two and a half hours had passed since I entered the hostage situation, and David had never — not once — taken his eyes off Melancon and me. It was like Ping-Pong, his eyes darting from one of us to the other and back again, Ping-Pong without stop. But as Melancon poured the $20,000 into Kathy's lap — 100 bundles each containing $200 — David looked down as if to count.

Bang!

Quicker than the eye could blink!

Melancon sprang at him like a jungle leopard. His left hand grabbed the hand holding the knife. His right hand cracked into David's mouth.

I lunged and pushed Kathy to the side. The knife clattered onto the black and white tiles of the floor. Something tore my left arm as the three of us rolled around the rest room in a mad, giant, death struggle. Behind us the S.W.A.T. bounded into the room, eight or ten of them, and with their help David was finally subdued.

Kathy was taken out to her parents.

David, in handcuffs now, was cursing. "I'll get you for this, preacher, I won't forget!"

An emergency medical service man was treating the gash on my arm. It wasn't very deep. Perhaps a belt buckle rather than the knife did it.

"You know what?" I asked the E.M.S. man who was bandaging my arm. "Two things happened today that have never happened before in my life."

"What are they, chaplain?"

"First, I have seen $20,000 in cash all at one time. And second, I've seen the inside of a ladies' rest room!"

CHAPTER 17

"Out of the Depths..."

11:05 A.M.

IT'S STRANGE HOW GOD WORKS.

Frances Pecora, a loyal and good friend over the past twelve years, was on the phone recently, and the subject came up.

"Father Pete, don't you ever get discouraged? Don't you ever feel down? My God, I don't know how you do it. You see so much of the seamy side of life—the gory, sickening part that very few of us see. How do you keep going—and smiling?"

As I said, it's strange how God works. Sure, I get discouraged. And I also get fed up at continually seeing man's brutality and inhumanity to man.

Like the other morning at 5:30 A.M. when I was called to a murder scene. They took me behind a cheap bar on South Rampart and pointed to the naked body of an attractive thirty-five-year-old woman who had not only been brutally raped, then stabbed to death, but whose genital area was cut and disfigured in a horrible, obscene way by her killer.

Or the time that a former altar boy, a kid from the Project named Louis, a kid whom I had trusted, let us down again. For the past six years, we had tried to help him. Time and time again. We had given him a job at the church; had paid his tuition through school; had counseled and advised him; had tried to be his friend. All this time, although I didn't know it then, he was stealing from the church and lying to us. When we caught him stealing for the last time, about three years ago, we had to let him go. There was no prosecution, just more words of advice—and fifty dollars to help him buy some new clothes.

Last week Joe Crespo, the lector at our early mass, left the altar and chased a thief who had tripped the alarm as he ran from the rectory. He chased him right into the arms of the First District police.

It was my former altar boy, Louis.

Like every other police chaplain in the nation, I wonder at times if our sick society is ever going to get cured. Or does it want to get cured? Are men and women ever going to begin to obey God's—and man's—laws?

Sure, I get disgusted with drugs and blood and cries and pain and lifeless bodies and raw violence. Sure, I get "down" from these and hundreds of similar experiences in this alive, inner-city parish.

But I don't *stay* down.

Because somewhere, at some time, there comes that happy burst of God's consolation: it's called *grace*. Reward. It's a good and a real feeling, and God shoots it to us just when we need it. And suddenly everything becomes worthwhile again.

I try to hang in there, hoping and praying that some one word I might have said to someone somewhere along the way—some one act of love or kindness that I might have done for somebody along the trail—might be the reason that even one person got closer to Jesus Christ—and to Christ's world.

And I know very well that the Lord doesn't give any-one—even police chaplains—burdens and downs heavier than they can carry.

I remember one special day when I was especially down—way down—when the Lord in His own wonderful and surprising way swooped in. All of a sudden everything looked worthwhile and bright again.

I had just returned from across the river. It happened in a section of New Orleans called Algiers. A police sergeant who was a good cop, a fourteen-year veteran and a close friend of mine, was sitting at his desk in the Fourth District station that morning. He typed a note, carefully arranged it, tidied up his desk, excused himself, and went to the rest room. There he pulled his revolver and put a bullet through his head.

After attending the sergeant, who died instantly, I drove to his home and broke the tragic news to his unbelieving wife and family. I spent the entire morning with them. When neighbors and friends drifted in later on, I returned to 411 North Rampart, weary, and with leaden heart. And all of a sudden I was very tired and discouraged and down and "beat."

I remember locking my office door and putting my head on my desk. I closed my eyes, using the day's unopened pile of mail as a pillow. I felt like I had to get away from the blood and the tears and the anguish, to get away from people screaming, *"Why? Father, why?"* And that's when I noticed the letter on top of the stack. It was from Angola State Penitentiary. It was from Phil Espositto, the "cop who went bad."

Phil was the policeman who had killed a man while under the influence of drugs a few years back. He had also tried to kill his girlfriend. And almost killed her baby.

When the judge handed Phil ten years at hard labor in the state penitentiary, I visited him just about every day in Parish Prison. He had trusted me; I wanted to do all I possibly could to warrant that trust.

I believed—as so often I have done—in this young man.

When the old prison bus lurched out past the gates of the New Orleans Parish Prison bound for Angola, about 120 miles away, with Phil, the former cop, chained to fifteen other convicts to begin his prison term, I went into action.

I phoned the chaplain at Angola and also talked to the warden and the assistant wardens there. I explained that Espositto was a cop—a good cop at one time. I told them that he had surrendered to me, that he trusted me, and that I promised to stick by him. I asked them if they would now help me.

Phil was assigned to work in the prison's mail room, with civilian personnel. He read a lot; kept to himself; avoided as much as possible the prison population. I sent him books on his Catholic faith; sent him a rosary and the St. Jude novena booklet from which he prayed daily.

Every morning I opened the *Times-Picayune* newspaper, expecting to see the blazing headline: EX-COP MURDERED AT ANGOLA.

But he wasn't.

I sweated out the ordeal almost as much as Phil did. He joined the prison program for people with drug problems. His easy-going personality, his desire to do his time, get out, and begin all over, and his belief in St. Jude's help were the driving forces that kept him going.

Over the rough, rugged months in prison, his faith in God and in God's forgiveness were key elements. Often in the evenings, instead of listening to the raucous Cowboy and Western music that was popular with other inmates, he went to the reading room and opened his Bible and read the story of the gentle Saviour and the adulteress. The words, "Let him who is without sin cast the first stone," appealed to him, as did those beautiful words of forgiveness, "Turning to the woman Jesus said, 'Nor do *I* condemn you. Go—and sin no more.' "

As I raised my head from the desk on that rainy, dreary afternoon, I stared at the letter from Phil Espositto. I ripped it open, and on the lined, yellow prison paper were some of the most joyous words that I had read in a long time—words that, once again, proved that God works in strange and beautiful ways.

Here is that letter, exactly as he wrote it:

> *May 20th, 1975*
> *73264-La State Pen.*
> *Angola, La.*

Father Peter Rogers
Our Lady of Guadalupe Church
411 North Rampart St.
New Orleans, La. 70112

Dear Father Rogers:

Today, I was interviewed by the La. Board of Paroles. The parole board, after reviewing my case, granted me a parole. I am scheduled for release on parole from La. State Pen. on June 7th, 1975.

Some people say the difference in life is, "what could have been, and what actually was." You have been the difference in my life. Starting with a telephone call from an unknown person, who stated he had killed and needed help. You learned that I was armed and influenced by drugs, yet you feared not for your life. You came to me armed with coun-selling and compassion, and brought me to my senses. Had it not been for you, others and possibly myself could have been killed.

Once arrested, you didn't forget me. Your visits during the initial phase of my confinement were a great help to me. Also, your letters were always a source of encouragement.

Most of the world's most famous people didn't receive the recognition they deserved until after their death. This is not true in your case. You are becoming a legend in your own time. One day the church will construct a statue in your honor. It will be a source of pride for those you have helped and a inspiration for the "Fathers" of the future.

The assistance you have provided me is greatly appreci-

*ated. I now have a second chance to become a productive
member of society and a loyal servant to our Lord.*

Sincerely,
Phil

Putting his letter down, I closed my eyes and breathed deeply. And whispered a prayer of thanks.

The whole world seemed well and alive again. Once again God's grace made it seem all worthwhile. I grinned as I walked past my secretary Fran, humming the old World War II song, "When the Lights Go On Again . . ." and took a beer from the fridge.

Settling in my favorite chair upstairs, I switched on the stereo and, lost in some very special, happy thoughts, leaned back and relaxed.

The telephone rang. It was Line 2.

"Car 30, this is Headquarters. They request you down on the river at the Thalia Street wharf. A fireman is trapped in a warehouse fire. Make it fast—on a Code 3!"